A Grand Sociology Lesson

ISBN: 978-1-94317-019-7

Cover Design: Jane L. Carman
Interior Design: Alyssa Hanchar

Typefaces: Arial, Avenir, and Chapparl Pro

Published by: Lit Fest Press, Carman, 688 Knox Road 900 North,
Gilson, Illinois 61436

Lit
Fest
Press

There are no rules.
festivalwriter.org

A Grand Sociology Lesson

KJ Hannah Greenberg

Table of Contents

Academies

Intermittent States

Regimes

Conduits

Preface: The Study of Society's Appendages

Critical analyses of social strata, of public institutions, of laws, and of media, help folks get the gist of how they can create additional goodness in their lives while suffering less. Clicked up a notch, this type of qualitative assessment, when put to verse, can capture the ecstasy of cultural creation, the pain of interpersonal failure, and the disharmony of negotiated vagueness.

A Grand Sociology Lesson, a book of ninety-four poems, articulates social experience. This assemblage mouths off about our shiny, waterproof practices as well as about our dull, unlaundered understandings. Accordingly, like the best of herbal bitters and like the least of conventional chemotherapy, A Grand Sociology Lesson is, in places, an uncomfortable read.

Yet, it is this book's irritating character that is its empowerment. Candy-coated troches, ornamental rhetorical doggerel, and good-tasting lessons in ethics fail to heal us of our less than desirable communal habits. Repurposing our words, though, can preserve us when we stumble with love, with loss, or with indecision. Whereas it doesn't matter how we review our experimentations with oak leaves, with dry ice, with nail liquor, or with baseball caps' orientation, it makes a great deal of difference how we prod our economic, our ethnic, and our psychological trials.

To wit, *A Grand Sociology Lesson* pokes without compunction. Let apologia remain the province of stout elitists, of persons whom appropriate little concern for the others' well-being. The rest of us must collectively grapple, poorly, or otherwise, with: rape, child abuse, the marginalization of elders, unemployment, debt, alcoholism, social exclusivity, housing shortages, insufficient medical care, and much more. Our discourse needs to get beyond worthless rodomontades. *A Grand Sociology Lesson* shows us that we ought to verbally nod at, whisper about, beep through expletives relevant to, and otherwise take possession of our commonplace affairs.

KJ Hannah Greenberg
Jerusalem, 2016

Introduction: A Grand Sociology Lesson

The poor's "muggers," "welfare recipients," "winos," "bandits,"
When multiplied, by millions of euros, dollars, yen,
Evolve as "innovative, manipulators of stocks,"
Morph, via social magic, to "ritualized hedonists,"
Transform as "retreatists," perhaps "bohemians."

Money's wishes grant "rebellious fascists' roles"
To selves relaxing, satisfied, on coconut beaches.
Meanwhile, we middle class, become "embezzlers,"
"Resigned bureaucrats," "skidding alcoholic," and "anarchists."
Our sandlot's just picture postcards.

Recall; when abiding, insolvent "citizens" become "workers."
In parallel, the rich weigh in as "civic leaders."
We middles, wash as "suburbanites," all chips, dips, plus cocktail parties.
Charming hostesses, beautiful mates, perfect children,
Distinguish our class.

Sometimes, we can cut expenses, dine clandestinely,
Push our offspring to accept "occasional jobs,"
Defy social bankruptcy without extra government helpings.
Such propinquity to power almost sates us.
Otherwise, there's unemployment checks.

Castes and Dynasties

All Manner of Rebellion

All manner of rebellion manifest down the street, where girls with dolls,
Boys pretending privates can trump coronels, cousins ribboned with
    tinsel,
Plus sweet marigold dust, spangled ponies, moons, promulgate the
    notion that felicitous
Ends result not from platapii marching on central hall, from
    psychological
Castration, or from the intermittent soligious evocation of social change,
Rather, from clean axiologies, expensive lawyers, spent gum, also tribal
    paint.

Given that physical outcasts most readily unify cohorts, instigate flash
    floods, lap dance,
Spoof cultural movements, burp without apology, die, we are well-
    advised to take heed
Of edacious camels, especially ones equipped with cameras, search
    warrants, billy clubs
As well as to regard, with caution, new studies in epidemiology, fatuous
    muskrats, senators.Be careful; contemporary exegesis leaves out
    mention of civilization's cracked
Core; most megalopolises spill yolk, white, shell, some tons of blood, over
    Gotham.

What's more, war's impact on gender issues, rape, genocide, especially in
    satellite
Cities, countryside pleasuredomes, additionally offworld campuses,
    result in argute realizations.
That paradise's VIP quarters lack glitter, violins, tourist dollars, willing
    horses, other plush fun.
Devoid of commonplace bibelots, ashabatis, cheese spread, and smokes,
    such domains'
Senescence, at best, draws Mayflies. Only inchoate leaders, rouge
    politicians, insolent teens, sailors,
Bankers appreciate digs as yielded. Final days are too much slick
    advertisement, draft, maybe mirage.

Thelma's Nursing Home

The bric-a-brac of cancer patients'
Tubes rivet high eyes toward
Her breast. He nurses.
Pink, gummy suction. Blue iris aura.
Esmerelda commands walker militancy.
Madanna and child look up,
Smirk away breakfast.

Hemmingway then Vonnegut remain
Poor company to cotton sheets
Starched beyond familiar America,
Reeking urine, mashed peas, arythomyacin.
Occupational therapy maintains
Dominos plus pot holders'
Little yarn on institutional frames.

Sirens bring hospital news,
Transfers and patients, all
Silvery monitors.
Elders' daycare charges draw
Cardboard pumpkin faces,
Marigolds from yesterday's newsprint,
Kissy puppy placemats.

Occasionally, cats kill, dragging
Carcasses 'cross winnowed yards,
By-passing bird-dappled chairs.
Misters Benson-Hedges sleep,
Three lungs between them.
Jackie, envisioning neat scotch, speaks
Gallic at Thelma's nursing home.

Mama's Mundane Witnessing

St. Sebastian's dachshund sniffs
Wide-eyed after pissing up Mrs. Shelly's impatiens. Strong-clawed
Back legs dig anemones; a clever front
Paw parts Shasta daisies.
I pick beer bottles from the lawn.

Cheryl's baby crawls on
Cement grass. Mama supports a mechanic's habit, soft curlers
Banana dabs, sometimes chocolate-ripple ribbons, while tall
Flags flap in Mama's mind.
Her sister, too, salutes armed services.

Mrs. O'Pickidy watches
Trash; pizza boxes, Trojan empties, days. Nights, she bowls
San Whatsies' Town Girls'
Team versus Carmine's House of Fashion.
Peter discounts lanes at nine.

The sidewalk half of the heart
Locket reminds children; practice spelling, fractions build neon fences near
Grand buildings, and remember Uncle Elmer's breakdown.
Superman's new edition challenges the yuppies.

Rorschach Blot Interpreted by an Automated Man

I spy bright tangerine tamberines
Resounding 'cross a salty sea
Such pretty pictures, that visual input,
Bring titihoya's veldt at once to me.

Summer's thrall lays magic outskins,
Whose caracal mitts run ever free,
Strumming merry thoughts gaunt like brushwood,
Evoking feral sanguinity.

I ponder giant, bicromatic wolverines,
Labyrinths tooled from shins and knees,
Look, there's a bit of auntie's sacrum,
Her biodet scents this broadsheet's breeze.

Observe! People flowers wilt too quickly,
Stalled awaiting numerous needs.
If only they would dip in solutes,
Attempt to preserve their weak species.

Flesh plus sinew affect misconduct
When silicon rots in wayward lees.
Even ink blots discern their falsehoods,
Articulate, ably, what 'bots already see.

I'm so Hungry I Could Sing about it:
Empty of Love and Money

An acquired taste, pizza plus
Cigarettes, also peanut butter.
Wedding invitation samples,
Contest forms for European
Honeymoons, gifts of bath towels,
Potential employers' communications
Fill my mailbox.

Sofa-bound, I smooth my comforter.
All such injuries lighten when
"Surprise me" means new sweaters,
Shiny trinkets, or discovering
Missing home repair magazines;
No one jives the media's fuss over
"Innovative" war toys.

The neighbors' passive aggression antics,
Akin to my partner's contact information,
Has been prostituted,
Made street-plain, on LinkedIn, Facebook, and Twitter,
Against the backdrop of the crystal bowl,
My grandmother passed down
To scent the decades with stewed fruit.
Had it not been for the quadriga,

Powered by dolphins,
Our collective, eidetic memory
Would have failed us while atramental
Ornamentation abounded, challenging
Affection-filled vessels' apparent release from
Pretended fidelities.

Cancer, political or otherwise,
Makes stalwarts, not ninnies,
Out of rational romance;
Serendipitously remaining heart's province,
Except when girlfriends are diagnosed pregnant;
Those times find steadfast trust disabled,
Reel in philogistons or burst upon contact.

Similar to plastic cups,
Thank-you notes and birthday cards
Can be ratcheted, in contrast
With a vacant dormitory room,
His mother's stepstool, advertised safe marriages,
Crumbled buildings' facades,
Also, administrative assistants' identities.

The untutored, ever willing to cover their heads,
To copy backward motes resembling
Research scientists' imperceptible finds,
Grow lax in promising,
Reluctant in committing,
Unable to leap tall relationships
In single bounds.

Maybe, they remember to share their lunches.
But, overall, the social strata remain confused,
Sleepy witnesses to fumbling intimacies,
To boundaries turned discrete for shame
To faith fashioned to fit
The upper echelons of logical positivism
When the unemployed populate Pittsburgh.

The Boondoggles of Debt: A Contemporary Lament

All the wisdom in counselors' fingers and in the heads of "true, good
    friends,"
Thwarted none of my fiduciary demons, despite the funds they marked to
    lend.

Whether consolidating or purely weighing just how big my gap might be,
There were no forthcoming greenback pulchritudes, from them, for now,
    for little me.

Although I've limned the applications of new bank cards of many hues,
Notwithstanding my high credit ratings, I've exhausted my long list of
    "things to do."

Calls to parents, pleas to bosses, even fresh restrictions on the kids' pocket
    money,
Yielded no further losses, but, likewise, gleaned no bonuses, tendered no
    honey.

Sometimes, I'd "won" by scoring some antique-like rates redolent of the
    1920s.
Other times, my liquid fortune brought me none, gifted me with no
    endeavors yielding plenty.

Given personal, multiple work shifts plus free-lancing, which makes me
    bleary,
And given that my rift persists, it's no wonder the entire mess crushes,
    razes, and leaves me weary.

The market's poor for remortgaging, I've naught left to retail on robust
    eBay,
In spite of years of education, my circumstances somehow shifted this way.

Accordingly, my dear reader, if you possess an inspired route,
Email it to me quicker than faster so I can facilitate my bailout.

Unemployment's Huffs and Puffs

Unemployment's huffs and puffs
Appear user-friendly when
Otherwise occupied by
Westerly shops' winds
Or saintly assemblages of
Inevitable social situations.

 Last gap measures largely
Terminate even fail-safe relationships
Whereas if, alternatively,
Presented front and center,
Such hagiography
Would disappoint even itinerants.

Habituations, alone,
Like those beyond my doorstep,
Blown down by antediluvian actions,
Succeed in landing
Chump change, temporary
Status, plus a little lunch money

The Pantyhose Horrors of Summer Internships

The summer of '79's facetious fun
Meant typewriter trauma, all manual,
Pantyhose horrors, thirty-five cent buses,
Faux pas built on office politics.
Most female interns floundered,
Stenography was a practiced art,
Supervisors were necessarily hung.

Jogging suits felt groovy,
Wall phone came in colors,
Coffee machines squirted choice,
Copy machines were dreams.
Big Bosses smiled at curled hair,
Painted lipstick, also mascara,
Executive lunchroom politics.

Work like a dog, think like a man,
Nod like a lady, fret like a child,
Expect people beyond PR,
To misunderstand (a lot).
Call shipping. Call shipping.
Read the newspaper,
Peruse dictionaries. Blow gum bubbles.

Call the west coast, Call the east,
Sneak a peak, without computers, at lists
Of your friends' fathers' promotions,
Twirl your extra office chair.
Get regular haircuts, manicures.
Memorize the company song.
Polish introductions, use white out.

These days, flat-screened, run-on realities dictate time sharing.
Gender preferences hide, other demographics slink, all LinkedIn aliases.
Working from home, bunny slippers, tea, hangovers, absorbs the
populace.
Maybe, perhaps, what if, a girlie elected an international commerce.
Would jet planes, transatlantic software systems, avatars suffice?
Contemporary time zones function as so much punctuation;
Interns, now, get paid to update technology, upload themselves.

Fame

When no one was looking,
I made a mark, on a wall.
Brightly colored, that line
Exclaimed my victory over
A small area.

Then it rained.
More precipitation, also entire seasons,
Passed in clouds. Originally
Grotesque, my smudge found peers,
Discovered equals.

A rising sun muted blotches,
Likewise mine. The war, too,
Blotted more than scored.
Support crumbled;
Society stood still.

Later, a backward leaning tree,
Ripe with incendiary stains,
Which had protected my smear,
Was felled for fuel.
Children were hungry.

A particular youth,
In a select ghetto,
Likewise hacked into securities.
No government device
Deterred her legend.

Current Regard for the Newly Not-so-Rich

Wayfarers dismiss all manner of crossings,
Involving gees, separate voices,
Or the wealthy, dispossessed.
Wanderers' tough, social fabric,
Taunt against recessions,
Hedge off perdition successfully.

That more moneyed souls, likewise,
Are fenced from happy bog or fern
Breaks no hobo's diatribe.
Further, those "sagacious" politicians
Yet fail to share oil drum fires
Around which simple men heat.

Today's trash out of McMansions
All empty ice cream cartons,
Inveterated backyard swimming pools,
Dusty chandeliers, maybe handsewn carpets,
Beats tom-toms taunt
Against a unified presence.

The middle class' mourning song, too,
Brooks no space for seasoned itinerates.
Learning from the rich customs of the destitute,
Not to make room for social "treasures,"
The average Joe rejects
Citizens with louche taste.

Pamela's Poem: Cabbage and Milk Thistle

Popular *brassica*, understood worldwide, grows in purple-white glory.
The farmer's wife, plus nearby villagers, hail its herbal wonder.
They gather visitors to taste, to celebrate, and to esteem.
"Cabbage" means "goodness."

Intermittently, on those same grounds, sappy stems sprout mottled,
    prickly.
Their nomenclature suggests nourishment beyond strong thorns.
Yet, few women dance festivals for spotted, toothy leaves;
Milk thistle's tolerated.

Unblemished persons, nonetheless, value briar blossoms alongside
    customary,
Sweet, global clusters as found in generations of mums' cook pots.
Such chaste puncture delicate fingers to reach for bristles.
Still, hurt surprises.

Meanwhile, daisies' kin notwithstanding, The Cultivator plows fields
    under.
Broken brindle bushes, alongside cole's leavings, suit His scheme.
Neither caboche nor cardoon remains extant.
Winter blankets both.

Because of a Woodland View

Don't buy because of a woodland view;
Property values can fall to obsolescence
When choice neighbors move. Plus,
The government harvests trees.

Hitching a ride to the stars
Leads to diesel burnout,
Also, to lost composite gloves floating
Beyond extravehicular activities' reach.

Parents' proffered advice about "please,"
"Thank-you" and "excuse me" become
Gratuitous teachings in cases where
Survival depends on knives or nunchucks.

Sticky Feasts ought not to be Second-Rate

Bad news to ascribe nefarious intent when accounting;
Simple incompetence often explains medical tests' hyponyms.
"Expert" relationships need distance, also fairytale stitching.

Drop cloths, likewise, splattered with limited pastel palettes,
Posit more than run of the mill anxiety, if viscous, odorless,
Tasteless, water-soluble worries, made existent pro forma.

Consider that women, ever fiendish in their multi-tasking,
Frequently follow bottom feeders to compromising positions
Better to buy a book, purchase a ticket, chew through fast food.

In balance, certain girls, straight away, can fence off despicable gents,
Drain malevolence from its root, mix that drivel with purl-like words
Strained from generic bonds, Marxist glues, semi-liquid mental states.

Know; rendering creatures for adhesives makes for back aches, shin
    splints, heartburn.
Preferable to skin Swedes, denude onions, dice enough rutabagas to forgo
    bookbinding.
Lanceless picadors can effectively grieve the loss of loved ones, fart, end
    infatuations.

Sometimes, children entering amusement parks, upon viewing
    megacosters' signs,
Believe they, too, can overcompensate for gravity by wishing, aloud, for
    world peace.
(Their grownups modeled imagination's efficacy over practical solutions,
    skipped homework.)

Unattended, those kids read junk mail, lick bruises, sip lice infestations,
    deny rheumatism.
Young, mentorless, they drift degrees of lassitude, chemically harden at
    instantaneous joints.

Despite feline signposts, ferocious resins, glistening gels, precious
   unctures, many expire.

Realize, juveniles are trained to recite, from nursery: fur ranks superior
   among tactile sensations,
Produces' main byproducts sit, stand, salute, in direct contention with
   social strictures,
Plus, vegetable gums, saliva, kinds of snot, form fixatives for the edgiest
   apertures.

Autoethnographic Writing Down Under

Such jubbily bits
From one joey, to the next
Constitutes campaigning.

It's easy to be understood as "ordinary,"
When vintage shades of meaning
Bring bouquets of words.

Other courtships' vantage points
Regularly identify with mama wombats,
But not infant marsupials.

They have yet to figure
That function's not superlative
To character or grace.

Enlightenment begins, in fact,
From frequent exchanges
Of the sympathetic kind.

Folks who exchange fashions
New, or in quick relief,
Miss truth through their gymnastics' emotions.

Such minds fail to weigh
Against insidious distractions
Or adrenaline's addiction.

Simply, attending to reality's underrated.
Most home proffer killer karate,
Analytic aerobics, and case-based reasoning.

The Amusement Park among the Steel Mills: Reminiscing over Pittsburgh

In the amusement park among the steel mills, where cotton candy, raw
	French fries,
Messy Slurpees, sell at least as well as do tickets to the Bobcat, the
	Thunder Bear,
The Mustang, next to the children's motorcar highway and the first aid
	station,
Alloy canisters, resting on cinderblocks, sing vitriol anthems.

Grande dame monoliths of production, such mighty manholes
Form mill workers, their families, twenty ethnic neighborhoods.
Assuredly, the chime of card clocks whisper aside of steel, iron, raw ore's
	din,
Calculate, conveniently, when nearby carousels might liberate enough
	small children

To merit taking a sick day or a timeout for some grandparent's "death."
In our district, while rickety dippers splash laughter, thick-gloved men,
Dressed in steel-toed boots, touting OSHA-sanctioned eyewear,
Check inventory, keep lines rolling, rolling, rolling.

Sometimes, parkland ponies fail to trot, after too many sticky hands
Pull manes, heel ribs, otherwise infuriate the beasts. Paused, they regard
Flocking ribbons of waste paper floating up toward our urban furnaces.
Dust's our Ides of Spring, our sooty snowfall, our cloudy forecasts.

We pay vendors handsomely for the right to ride. Yet, many monkey faces
Mean to regard our homes like fun houses. Outsiders never learn
That arcade miracles, perogies, Italian loaves, all sell two for one
Before closing time. They're too engrossed with winning on the midway.

Vim

Neighborhood Nuisances through Cats' Eyes

Squirrels busied with their crazed devices tend to miss humans'
   obsequious acts;
Most nutters adjure efforts, creating caches grand enough to satisfy
   viziers.
Jejune in their sensibilities, with homes all the more resembling aerial
   gopher holes,
Those flying vermin insist that without turf markings, all backyards
   remain their imbroglios.
Invidious others, after all, are plentiful in the arboreal community. No
   exceptions.

Indoors, diffident two-footers, attach ells to collars, proof bird feeders
   against theft,
Try to erect unnatural barriers among species. Even the family basset
   howls when furry prowlers
Dance. For sorts who suck on pearls at weddings, such acting out
   succeeds in avoiding
Choleric rodents' remonstrations, also the disapproval of mothers-in-law,
   bounty hunters,
Clerics, despots, plus kindergarten teachers. Wee critters' polemics rebuff
   most predators.

Consider that actions inimical to the interests of backyard fauna elsewise
   overwinter
Extravagance, youth, pregnancy, and increased tariffs on bubblegum. If
   sparrows would only
Volunteer themselves to enervate before kitty cats' dishes, fat toms, lazy
   queens, smug kittens
Might unsettle nearby bipeds by engaging in vainglorious strutting,
   commonplace purring, farts.
Meanwhile, perfidy remains the province of felines great and small, tree
   rats notwithstanding.

Bent Reeds

Bent reeds, at first wind,
Anguish from daydreams soured;
Their frail, inclusive tetany marks fey loss.

Elsewhere, little crocuses, saffron flowers, all,
Prophesize summer's magnetic resonance, drought,
Provide low beauty to otherwise spun meaning.

Tuesday Night at the Student Union, 1979

Jim Kahn sneezed four slices of mushroom pizza.
Later, his briefcase made love to peace treaties.
Sarah Bernhardt dropped her cellular phone,
Spilling French fries on Elvis.
Sammy crumpled more paper.

Behind pages of rhinos and zebras,
Medical schools signed off, leaving
No anthem. Quaaludes' omnipotent
Smile shook calculus, physics plus particle
Chemistry, ran amok within her. He frowned, face first.

Salt scattered the length of plastic cans plus
The breadth of napkin canisters.
Mustard dollops decorated remnants.
Voices from the cheerleading squad declared
Two points. More bad rock and misguided weather while
A brunette slept.

My quarter rolled, Dinking after dropping . . .
Under recycled benches.
Two rows away. Fraternity belching.
More coffee.
Matchbook cover numbers. Straw darts.

Shakespeare's Third Act completed.
Nintendo for nine cents. Empty paper sugar packets.
A misplaced sock. More note cards.
More coffee. More musak. German Grammar.
Es ist. New York Times crossword puzzles.

Das Zeit.
50% off remaining burgers.
Folded notebooks.
Tomorrow's cheat sheet left behind.
Tomorrow's cheat sheet left behind.

Versey: The Wilds of Advertising

Encircling streams flit reeds, reflect sun,
High low, where hummers breed, suck colorful tatters,
Tear down expectations, revise marketplace events.

Survival, no matter one's homes or natural inclination,
Trumps, until some fashion-linked zephyr brings upward drafts
To irregular seasons, causes erosion by means of confabulation.

Then sky fish, which never lived in camouflage, preferring
Penthouse comfort, chirp, whisking away nursery-like hushing,
Perform prestidigitation, also, other tweaking of customers' minds.

'Cause certain truths, multiplied, when located in aether, if pleasantly
Spiced, or otherwise tastefully served up, function, make presumptions,
Falter to fold, crease caladon edges, wrinkle masks plus tails.

So goes until cock's crow, whether neon or, perhaps, in bytes;
Carefully placed propiniquities laud without criticizing,
Strike fast and dirty against organized notice, fracture fixed wit.

The Smell of Water

The smell of water in an iron sink portends
Fictions of yesterday's lunch, also our obstreperous
Love-filled cupcakes, coffee, cream cheese sandwiches.

Such a sine qu non as ours often requires
Primary care providers to access chat rooms,
Avoid pabulum projectiles, smile frequently.

In a family's comings and goings, details like
Dog hair on the sofa, first class letters, toothpaste lids,
Get lost in the lugubriousness of failed diapers, postage stamps, sleet.

Calls to home, from teachers, too, raise
Specters of exaggeratedly gloomy prospects;
Riven social comments were all that was needed.

Our completion requires careful replacement
Of worn ribbons, spilled cereal, shed tears
Whether the ingredients get concatenated or not.

Telephone Love of Decades Past (A Carol)

My passing thoughts linger, frame you.
Love's snapshots flicker in review.

Your equations' call abided,
Certain company's divided,
By Ergo's links, such noise's quieted,
Sums mutually construed.

Heart sports flourish, occasions find
Voices rub simple, 'near always entwined
Miles rules, but feelings bind;
Telephones join the voice of two.

My passing thoughts linger, frame you.
Love's snapshots flicker in review.

Across the mountains our words dance,
Not fused by sight, they're our romance.
Your nod, your smile, your special glance,
Animated our set hitherto.

Now, in dreams, our fingers touch,
They link, they hold in lovers' clutch,
With words we grope, we stroke as such,
Greater times when we're renewed.

My passing thoughts linger, frame you.
Love's snapshots flicker in review.

Civilization's "Little Words"

Little words, birds of meaning flying above anathema foes,
Pulling high from fiends wishing to quench, to bite, to consume,
Hope, celerity, burnished essence. Such representatives, as enjoy world
Rights, make poor snacks for nefarious beasts; usually, glitter
Gets stuck in maws, makes throats constrict around joyful song.

Singular sorrows cost many apples whereas entire lots of ebullient acts
    are cheaper.
Scapegoats, mountain sheep, other bovine, stupidly substitute for human
    hubris.
Few soldiers, minus their jousting sticks, sharp pointy things, guns,
    willingly
Inculcate bravery; rather, their most eleemosynary work involves
    prisoners.
Sans elevated imprimatur, battlefield cowboys live no better than
    common sparrows.

Ignorant of mindful thought, largely, folk tilt at effluvium, wave hands
    before lightening,
Run crying when hail, snow or raindrops hurl earthward. Justice's back
    pocket protects
No fools, only opens admission to civilian's fulminations, then quickly,
    seamlessly closes.
Armed forces are no longer successful in perjuring enemies. The enlisteds'
    untruths make
Governmental tomfoolery unnecessary. Budget cuts apply, affront
    lawyers, not keg partiers.

Round, Pop, Shout

Round, pop, shout over aspidistra jungles.
Pout when adolescents dare fail to coruscate.
Don't let it show, though, if fire departments,
Principals, even janitors, interfere. Hug social media.

Hovering near chemistry lab closets fetch nothing;
Sowing file upon file of empty advertising, too, lacks.
Only ombre-toned hair, half matted in phony dreadlocks,
Or partially shaved from heads, can resuscitate dead networks.

Nonetheless, dreaming's still free. Fantasy costs zilch.
Riding up and down department store escalators, likewise
Especially in condemned buildings, where fire trucks' actions,
Resulted in weak and helpless moments, bring about taffy pulls.

Camphor, lithium amide, sulfur are susceptible to exploding.
There's little chance nose pickers ever evolve into champions;
The underdogs' guardians are required to possess clean hands, feet.
Alternatively, they employ katanas to cut down bullies, spread peanut
        butter.

Elsewise, goodie two shoes sandwich themselves on donkeys' markabs,
Inhale stuff like ketamine, chew betel leaves, belch, perhaps flatulate
        regularly;
No rescue comes from nonruminant animals chewing phytates, spitting
        at strangers.
Stumping, though, busies bodies, even impacts those trussed in
        morphsuits, gives thrills.

Accordingly, legerdemain among natives tired of kissing begets blithe
Relationships, casts off emotions, possibly removes unwanted progeny.
Considers as best actors, those in groups who repeat again, again, again.
Claim others' words as theirs, hiccup when locked in latrines. It happens.

My Backyard Squirrels

My backyard squirrels,
Dumpster cats to a one,
Know more about high-toeing
Than does any Nashville giant.

Dead or alive,
Those toms plus queens
Serve up homage to bone, to blood,
Maybe even to occasional viscera.

Why is tabby blessed with voice and vice
When retirement brings rot
To other species?
There's something in those whiskers.

Some sunshine stains
Such thoughts 'til tomorrow.
After all, Larry was more nimble
Without the candlestick.

He Thrives while I'm Exsanguinated

He thrives while I'm exsanguinated; buckets beneath, lines above.
Middle aged, too, he needs no needle hyjinks, suture speculation, or loose
    change.
Those verbal fangs suffice to draw blood.

I merely espoused the vicissitudes of the mass media; likewise, unplugged
    some such devices.
Chocolate drops, sour tea, also penny buns, need to replace screens,
    modems, intercoms.
Convergent media makes for untidy snacking.

Meanwhile, she kicks golden dust, that sonika-child; lives as a fresh,
    enlivened generation.
Wombtime ill-sufficed to integrate regular rules' litany into her psyche.
Such individuals, empowered, make dust of elders' diatribes.

We form family; our textured veracities get served up alongside each
    morning coffee.
Concurrently, extra hours of sleep escape us, young and middle-aged, alike.
Gasping, evermore, we recognize the confluence of domestic factors.

Israeli Jasmine, Manicured

Jasmine, hedge-high, bordering a beachfront bungalow,
Slung itself along the Mediterranean, in a land
Shaded by disputes of international stature, grows.

Pigeons, gray, brown-red, also white,
Opined witnessing to local, pedestrian issues
Missing all traces of ocean tranquility, take flight.

Conch shell inhabitants, tiny, maybe thumbnail-sized,
Chorused periodic flowery, feathery, or dysfunctional flash
Rumoring natives as no more than immigrants or tourists, slide.

Certain civic cases, cached by multinational requests for mollification,
Spun "insights," didn't offer counterpoints to foreign correspondents
Habituated in gifting bad press to residents, erupt.

Yet, all the beauty of sky-filled vistas, chain smokers, darting lizards,
Cedars, acacias, myrtle, oleaster, cypress, box trees, likewise elm,
Waylaid by dint of ill-intended, external aloquoting procedures
Designed to trump the population, continues on, unabated.

Forget Elastic: A Midlife Melody

Forget elastic, also tentative explorations of dressing rooms; there's no tomorrow after
Church bells peel funeral dirges for single digit sizes. Such stay forever with the devil.

Rather, run amok among ordinary confections; it's better to indulge in gibber
Than to suffer ringworm, dysentery, other raucous diseases, also dislodged thoughts.

Advertisements that affect cures for unrecognized problems, like kudzu, the bejeweled eyes
Of grasshoppers, bumblebee's comings, goings, and feuds, slyly reproduce without legislation.

Old fashioned common-sense, new-fangled funding, the "signature" of elements,
Belong in museums, mayhap to line polyarchs' walls or our wallets. At fifty, break free!

On Her Birthday, That Threshold of First Roses

On her birthday, that threshold of first roses,
All ruby or magenta-shaded, scented,
(Unlike blooms these forty years latter),
We got silly with charades, danced performances,
Made ingenious skits, bubbled forth festive singing.

Cakes, nowadays believed "old-fashioned,"
Then grew frosting flowers, turtles, goldfish,
While neighbors' spangled little girls,
Their cares maybe more on jumping stones,
Than keeping party dresses clean, laughed.

Safta, too, often visited us those Junes,
Just as days were long, nights cool, gardens special,
Crocheting Barbie skirts laced through with Carpathian
Magic; each pulled loop extending equinox kisses,
Firefly enchantments, ice cream truck music.

Weeks before school let out, under pearly skies,
We rode bikes bedecked by streamers,
Played kickball, four square, freeze tag,
Whispered to our dear, collected friends,
Even stayed awake giggling at the stars.

Fifty is Years Old Enough

Fifty is years old enough to sprout white hairs,
Wear elastic-waisted skirts, sing off-key,
Additionally, to rub eyeglasses clean on trousers,
Handkerchiefs, tablecloths, maybe also slightly-used linens.

Fifty is years old enough to read *Tarzan*, *Rumpelstiltskin*,
King Kong, *Little Red Hood*, *Captain America*, while exclaiming
Such tiff surpasses Camus, Hesse, Kierkegaard, Sartre, ought
To be taught, instead, come next term's Freshman English.

Fifty is years old enough to need memories held fast,
Gripped tightly, bound and rebound in spectacular narrative,
Captured as parenting topics, while children rehearse flight,
Even when such assemblages can causes initial difficulties.

Fifty is years old enough to question one's outermost valances,
Severing, perhaps, current loops of convergent communication,
Reassembling habituated consumption of personal services,
Especially those helps understood as portraying vulnerability.

Fifty is years old enough to take steps toward fleshy prowess,
Define physical goals, strategize corporeal plans, actualize body changes.
Gravity gets forgotten in the company of wisdom lines, silvered fur, fat,
Bumps, spots, warts, hangings, danglings and other marks of age's beauty.

Given a Chair

Given a chair, we might just touch the stars,
Take for neighbors sun and moon, sprint among asteroids.

Otherwise, plastic flags, paper litter, the squeak of second seat clarinets,
Will have to sate us sartorially, must suffice as bursury to our elucidations,
Maybe, ought to kowtow, as well, to such atavism as pokes requests
    through realizations.

After all, young, pony-tailed toddlers do not cease nor desist from
    fingering, pulling
Seams on their trousers, lint off their shirt jacks, discovering oily sweat,
    tinfoil, chocolate.
Humanity's hope remains winter's carrots, guppy harvests, sinecure jobs,
    fog, glitter, snow.
Piccolos toot sweet, yet leave us longing for new dimensions in taxes, rain,
    also childbirth.

The Fullness of Aging: Autumn's Showy Bounty

Bottle gourd or butternut breasts,
Watermelon abdomens,
Hair like leeks gone wild,
As well as vines of veins plus capillaries,
Designated to pulse, surface, burst,
Beyond the staid domains of "maid" or "madame,
Evidence crones' shiny new growth,
Elders' budding in sports, arts, science, love,
Midlife mamas' filling of fields better than can youth.

Such natural female finery as never experienced before
Decks gardens, gated communities, moreover hospitals,
Proves, again, that the fullness of age necessarily,
Also successfully, flouts lesser spans' decorations.

Academies

The Empyrean, Principality of Young Ages

Her hands are too small for
Reaching the typewriter return.
The toilet lever's as impossible as
Those poker playing housewives

Winning twice; child of abuse, and
Alcohol's strange moons,
She's pure fire, that empyrean,
Principality of young ages.

"Retarded:" Another Spoil of Child Abuse

Individual esteem teeters where
Social development's just a jewel in higher climbing.
Too few among the ambitious
Realize real ramifications of rubricing.

Those sagacious sorts grasp and spout that severe impairment,
Triggered by nights of shouting, slapping, stomping,
At offspring, at spouses, at pets, cleft days,
Impossibly resulting in fractured juveniles.

They lecture that familial fiduciary crises,
Parental drugs or alcohol,
Rough neighborhoods, sickness, all
Route innocents to emergency rooms.

They point out how
Red lights, whistles blaring,
Announce unmentionables, the sort
Captured on x-rays, records, police videos.

Later, "tonsillectomies of the hypothalamus,"
Performed by their well-intentioned social workers,
City administers, undereducated clergy,
Bring about further breakage.

Consider that while spacesuit bladders are rubber,
Little boys' heads were never meant
To resist harsh cosmic vacuums,
Oceanic atmospheres, clinical evaluations.

Pajamas, messy shoes, peach pit games, submarine imaginings,
Ought, instead, fill moments where
Children labeled "developmentally handicapped"
Could have thrived, would have grown straight.

No soul needs to be constrained to sweeping
Civilization's discarded bits into self-supplied bins.
Fairy dust costs too much for happily ever endings.
The youthful "derelict" has long been a collaborative project.

Piaget's Sagacity

Piaget, stuffed to his buttons,
But otherwise comfy,
Remarked, to established others,
"Childish wisdom
Anamorphisizes intentionally."

In contrast, select life volumes,
Unbound by words on paper,
Or screen, glisten,
Wet, like flocks mustered
For branding.

Human creation's purposefulness
Channels need, unless deterred.
Sometimes, random hibernacula
Of imaginary hedgehogs
Go wild on marshmallow fluff.

Whereas all manner of Furry conventioneers
Demonstrate positive social function,
Their deviance's bottled for distilling.
Such moral reasoning assumes
Headstands, without involving cartwheels.

Ambiguities require night feedings,
Daily waterings,
Occasional shearing.
Axiological absolutes only
Glow safely at roundup.

An Adolescent's Didactic Lament:
Round Pegs, Square Holes

You teach no circles, explain no diameters, work radii-free,
While my growth's never a quadrilateral, ever all right angles;
By no means, will I form ninety degrees at every corner.

On no account, can I learn sides, or supplementary comprehensions
Concerning standard coordinates. Realize, please, I'm rendered helpless
By vertices, as well as loathe norms which automatically spew postulates.

Responding with yelps, demanding length squared, makes probable
    nothing.
My answers require circumferences, additional centers, cones,
Alternatively, metric tensors, Gaussian curves. In fact, I might spit

If authorities bring reprimands, castigations, chastisements, or
Take away my garden shears, exclusive of providing crayons,
Modeling clay, stuffed bears, ancient Aramaic, hyperbolic conventions.

Necessarily, I sneer through bites of cake, despise your carrots, silly diets,
    also
Euclidean rules. Too bad on such foodstuff. Regrets regarding the menu.
Fixed inconsistencies seem puree; teens feed on plausible
    deconstructions.

So, when you show no rounds, I'll draw no squares. Plate those
    incommensurabilities.
My geometry remains "elliptic," or, on alternate Tuesdays, "parallel."
Your contradictions linger inexplicably, persist as wearyingly low in
    provisions.

Little Mustangs among Older Friends

After the storm, mountains' dread, dark frontage
Grimly regards valley lambs, kids, calves.
Those newborn droves scamper lily-like in dewy cover,
Acrobat among butterflies, balance maws
Full of sun, sweet grasses, little forbs, sometimes gorse.
Such wild babies prance until falling down exhausted.

Their ancient vanguard teeters on burly legs, his heft's
Wrapped in misshapen fur. Such short-flamed breath
Knew life, as frequented by keepers' great abundance.
These days, he whinnies protections fashioned from air, earth, water.
The herds' hillside poverty denotes nothing, zilch, naught.
Grazers so young need milk, grooming, dry beds, minding.

Birth, work, leisure, death's cosmic wheel recognizes
Escape only from cataract-eyed does or crippled bucks.
Youngsters sort triflings differently; when human ropes, halters lope by,
Youths merely lift their heads, momentarily stop
Ambulating among clover, frolicking with bumblebees,
Swatting at invisibilities.

Stroppy Urchins

Stroppy Urchins, all twee among tourists, call out for clothes,
Pave self-promotion in alleys, on streets, steady among boulevards.
Etiolate brats, accustoms to sweat shops, they beg bread, pester gypsies,
Commonly sift among urban cruft for invisible diamonds, rubies, emeralds.

Such social tetany brings bolshy, sometimes exasperatingly belligerent,
    faculatives,
Strolls wee persons 'round would-be bourgeoisie, nabs purses, filches
    pocket change.
Almost never, however, does it stoop to slit a throat; safer robbery will do.
Plus, obstreperous coppers are known to find pleasure in jailing hoodlums.

Now and then, brogues rest. When bounty's beyond reason, including:
    plimsolls,
Chatelaines for opening post boxes, rusted lugers, tame budgies,
As well as coins faced with etchings of ancient krakens, life's good.
Yet even those catches get revealed as more superficial glitz than social
    currency.

Australian Kennels

Alone, a boneless dog,
Without stick, toy, or shoe,
A beagle's velvet points
Not toward cars or rabbits,
But splintered bits, mosaic beauty,
Honeysuckle-shattered maps,

Winging away again
Without a hug,
A rug's worth of thin, worn reminiscing.
Small, smelly traces of golden wattle.

Daydreaming past people-paged creation,
Considered, in reputable circles,
As lonely, loveless.
Sad, blue, sans home or blackwood sanctuaries.

Pals purport to vibrate joy, merriment,
Levity. Like life, to wit, squirrels plus skunks
Reemerge at sunrise, spurring relevant images.
Jetsam's no use for gleaning gems' ordinary parts.

Poetic truth, though, gleams beyond caged
Fancies from protected lists' sentries,
All fur and skin, wasting when
Sufficient prowess lacks.

A butterfly's detached avarice
No more threatens than spring raindrops.
Sadness rolls eventualities
Into pink and gold creatures,
A light silver banksia,
Makes no more miscreants of hounds.

Some Cranium Treasures Sit Derelict:
Reasons to be Mindful of Children

Towering others,
Noising off on various windowsills,
Interior spaces, plus outdoor "rooms," forget
Youth's facility with memory.

Princess bathrobes, tiaras, coin girdles,
Others, constructed by financial packages,
Bind asymmetric azimuths beyond
Wee ones' heads.

Reach, which clears resolve,
Wearies halfhearted landforms,
Fatigues indolent responses, kills
Commitment in children.

Such grief,
Impacted again and again,
Pierces hope, faith, trust; creates
Fragmented belief.

Discounting adults, otherwise unaware,
Form fluvial masses,
Fail to recall some cranium treasures sit
Derelict.

School Norms: Innocents Enough to be Eaten Alive

State systems gobble innocents enough
To fill fields with better cotton.
Subjected to wild manners of screed,
School children wither not from sun,
Shatter not from wind,
But slough off their belief in truth when
Harms results from stormy diction.

Little hearts can not grapple,
Ought not to defend themselves;
Discounting rhetoric's not the stuff of
Love, advice or erudition.
Nonetheless, small heads are bought and sold
At small profit; just marks in officials' ledgers,
Mere words for politicians.

Probity demands vituperation
When purity's offered in exchanged for agitprop.
Yet, chaste revenants grow in number.
Too many eponymous louts freely forward
Insensate destruction.
It's not merely teachers who quake;
The next generation, too quavers.

Ill-Planned Legacies

Young life's anguish, at some energetic level, unavoidably gets mired with
superstitions,
The subsequent analysis of which shows social guardians' imperfect gneiss.

Eponymous to a fault, sanctioned sanity suggests protecting against attack
or injury.
Nonetheless, upper strata repeatedly insist the onus rests on mundane
workings.

Cultural norms, it seems, at the cost of greater decay, select worldviews
powered by gas,
Also uphold the stoichiometry of bilious postulations married to pomp.

Whereas selling out, based upon sculpted assumptions, provides odd relief,
even laughter,
Unplanned pit stops, plus tantrums from lonely children, prove otherwise.

Annular ideas, however incipient, explore, evoke and champion the cheat;
huffy,
Gross displays of caring, of eluvium still wash up which stigmatize dogs
and gin.

Fug Music

Street vendors, all giddy-up and go in clown-colored accoutrements,
Balaclava, gloves, rainbow scarves, aviator glasses, also striped ties,
    prevaricate.
They hawk razors, shoelaces, lollipops, pickled watermelon, dope, to
    middle class sorts.
Additionally, they spin harsh sounds; notes all jangly, melody lines absent,
    rhythms clarion.

Whores, pigeons, alley cats, strut most mornings, weaving fur, garbage,
    mud, cruel facts,
Hard protests, missing hunks of hair, laughter, lawlessness, sequins, beer
    cans, select evils.
Alto outside, tenor indoors, such felines scream when pinched, pulled at,
    or otherwise stymied.
Urban chanting's become a maddening thing, discordant grates, complex
    pitch, but no swing.

Eat Merrily: A Little Girl's Cacophonous Tastes

Stuffed children, eat merrily
Rainbow-clad, troughs,
Everlasting spangle.
Singing, singing, singing.

If houses were of bubble gum,
Streets of sweetened salts,
Oceans filled with cherry pop,
Lakes of chocolate malt,

Then Sally Saunders' pillow-based
Allergy, fitted beyond feather tickles
To shapes, stripes, and mass' collective softness
Might source, again, her nose to new neighbors.

Marshmallows, I assume,
The rocking horse plus jungle fowl.
Deciduous dancers in the breeze,
Would petrify, silenced, at sugary hours.

Sniffling, sad, Sally yearned,
Yielded and acquiesced
To rest her head on something better.
She screamed for a bolster.

Plentiful dead poultry,
Patient to a number
Basking patent leather sunshine
When half a cork crumbs chocolate crumb.

Common folk, those ginger bread,
Could have no teeth to chew
If it happened that they did,
Cavities all through!

Mightily miffed, Sally supposed
Sleepy sacks meant someone merited
Histamine-free drifty days;
Darlings needed in other ways.

Changes come and children know,
Oracles rise as soothsayers go
Truth reflects what
Wisdom should.

Sally sullied many stores pursuing dreams of more
Stones, cements, ornaments to cushion her sweet head
Turtle shells and cocker bells made mad our little girl.
The fruit's rotten 'neath the sheet, but her appetite's been thrilled.

Past the Halflings' Village

Far away,
Past the Halflings' village,
An old man,
Dry apple-wrinkled,
Peels a pear with a weathered pen

Knife-like, his anger is not
To be caught in words
Or fixed in crayon.
Unlike deep purple/crimson/aqua passion,
His hurled sand and stone
Hit deafening madness,
Depend on the vagarities
Of road conditions.

Fakes find fault.
Reindeer prefer solid ground,
Especially if singing the springs green.

Dreamy midwives of sunshine tend
Creation's metamorphosis,
Even during parkway commutes,
Making paper bag lunches taste
Like so many snowflakes.

When we seek and destroy,
To perform among acacias,
Ignoring red river gums plus eucalyptus'
Troubled streams,
Jeremy and Candace tend to run away.

The Gift Shop Woman-cum-Housekeeper Mama

The gift shop woman-cum-housekeeper mama nee' childcare provider,
Smiled blandly. My daughter clutched thumb and finger, squeezed
My hand until I dropped the leash, completely, of her giraffe on wheels.
Better to join her chase of white geese than to read *The New York Times*.

Thirty-seven country miles later, in a minivan outfitted with loot, I ate
    pink, yellow, white
Sugared bunnies while she wailed the inadequacies of babysitters. My
    respite, with her father,
Meant to melt my memories of my Daddy's fingers crawling arms, legs,
    chest was rot. Like my
Solo flights, that partner time, baby making, even confectionery
    intoxications, did not help.

If only adolescence had been honeysuckles plus lilac. While I tucked her
    beneath quilts
I dreamt on fantastic childhoods, imagined innocent cuddles, wished for
    impossibilities.
Auto wrecks, cancer, disasters happen. Nice people, community pillars,
    became perpetrators.
Parents morph to villains. I watched my hands during bath time, was
    hyper-careful diapering.

Paying therapists, researching nannies, installing cameras remains
    naught, zilch, nothing
Against yesterday's infested minds run amok. So, while Lovely howled at
    duck ponds,
I killed my intestines in the backseat. Later, we reconnected as though
    sunlight, alone,
Not storms, not mud, not road debris, could form the substance of small
    vacations.

Anteros' Celadon Whirligig: A Lecturer's Antique Regret

Twelve long minutes after shutting the chapter on acids and alkalines,
My reaction, not the least oxidized, was to spurn those myths of flesh,
Silicon-linked, carbon-based, or otherwise. Greek figureheads, akin to
    undergraduates
Full of ale, hearty opinions on gams, plus three days' worth of stairwell
    graffiti,
Most seminal in their ability to conjure synergistic thresholds beyond
    which no
Made-in-honor sample of salts or others soluble substances might trickle
    sufficiently,
Prove nothing when faced with worn planchettes, panaflexes allegedly
    gilded or Arrow-like cuspidors. Sparta, Athens, Crete provided but
    stoichiometric answers
While today's grimy spindles of department chairs, also, sharpen no one's
    ken.

Professors seeking promotion over and over again offer syncretisms,
    whirligig Rhetoric crippled by lust-filled treaties, desirous tomes,
    differentiated tributes to staid
Tenure committees. Sadly, such riotous rites of come hither-kissy face,
    moreso
Than even the most sublime intermolecular forces, bond not demigods to
    mortals.
Rather, they create attractions more masochistic than beneficent, more
    masque,
More groveling than merit. Even pandering Hellenics, fond of Eros,
    Anteros,
All cupidic in actualization, knew better than to squander esteem to
    mendacity.
Antique affections, psychic, logistic or pathos-based, spewed departed
    mystery.
Their parabolic washes, true "old-fashioned" romance, meant "righteous"
    chemistry.

Intermittent States

Hardly any Cosmic Answers at the Universe's Hub

Today, the center of the universe farted rainbows,
Which, in turn, morphed into broken rays of light,
Also handsome reflections of pixie dust, unicorn
Fetlocks, gryphon scales. The best friend of our
Neighborhood's chief chimera scampered by, whistling
For the most minor of invisible dolphins to glide alongside
His select phosphorous hedgehogs.

Later, a sort of friendly gelatinous beast ate my capybaras
Since those rodents were perpetuating wanton seed dispersal,
An enlarged disease vector, plus burning indigestion.
Some alley cats, phasing in and out of the area, exclaimed,
Accented by no small amount of concern, that bengaline,
Yesterday, was proclamation-worthy, but, presently, merits
Less gold than do walrus tusks.

As well, contemporary crustaceans, which swim, pay for mobility,
Excepting barnacles that remain ugly, worldly survivors,
Running ever amok among fuss, storm, pollutants. Cartouches accordingly
Discovered in sunken ships bring bullion, television specials, fans,
To men, women, plus critters, better off drowning in ale, bitters, wine,
Alternatively, attending toilets, shoplifting pantyhose, cleaning ray guns,
Yet always seeming able to avoid housework.

Cat fiddlers, blue moons, lost horizons, sourced from beyond,
Under half-functional neon strobes, meet, dance, swig, belch,
Hum shanties, cuss, kick back powdery substances, glow low-voltage
Until zero event vespers, those most suited to interplanetary radiation,
Boil out all evidence of protocol, wanderings, sluiced rubies, aronia berries,
Separate any references to galactic thesauruses, hidden gifts, monocles,
Especially directions to cosmic answers.

If Birds were to be Believed

If birds were to be believed,
Home birthing would make more sense than
Most modern measures of cutting or drugging.

If we listened to cattle's low,
Funding would spill easier than
Pay per SEO words or term papers.

If grasshoppers were heeded,
Planted truths would multiple faster than
Convergent media cottoning, including their picking among principles.

If we dared to reinforce personal event verities,
Taking responsibility would become simpler than
Combing hair with fingers or brushing teeth without paste.

Hitherto, birdsong, reliable agronomics, media ethics, interpersonal
        niceties
Remained rarer than instances of assorted rhetorical styles of dead,
        Greek orators.
After all, commerce's kudzu reaches no friendly tentacles or praise toward
        common folk.

Regard Carefully

Regard carefully this complex, not-yet-fully automated universe,
Which sets its spin among cosmic desiderata, space stations, love.
Cost-effectively filling, embracing, controlling, compensating
Rapacious others wanting no allowance, space, concession.
Imagine permitting nothing riven to fly, to swim, to walk, to be adjured
By couples' voluble hankerings. Such "civilizing" quickly collapses.

Hence, regarding commonplace orbs of feelings, also crystalline tears,
These get fondled too frequently. In craving deep, recondite grottos,
Our private mise en scene crumbles. No clement judge jumps up,
Develops avengers for our shared cold, muted walls. Our bulwarks
Stifle heaven's harmonies, even staccato, acciaccatura, *semifusa*.

Hence, where birdsong echoes, when fires' animation casts
Shadows along the edges of ethereal luminescence, clouds hope,
Somber, effete mortals stoop, conquer nothing, maybe cry.
No more than external churning remains to mark like coruscations.
Glitter's threshold is a short-lived cupidity. We erred with prolix texts.

So, life passes. Birth washes death washes continuity. We disappear.
Unkempt children bend, break. Colts bolt to stallions and then
Horses get shot. Mimsy thoughts become the calumny of legend.
Most existence warrants no kindred asperity. Under twinkling stars,
Man, beast, machine, alike, fade sooner or later, pay back creators.

Term Choice

Measured motes, incorrectly inserted,
Change the whole scene, ruin
An entire play.

Your tongue quicks my imagination
Until such words sour, dropping
Larva feelings.

Thereafter, motivation's coordinates vary
Per mood, menstruation or mentation. Guard
Your speech.

Certain Parameters

Certain parameters' brief fictions might get played out
When undertakings, trounced by sparrows, wrens, select jays,
Surge with songs of desolate places, evil sensations, analytical beadles,
Vast tracts of memorized texts.

Portended invertebrate victories, thereafter, could be minimalized
According to rare energy pockets, motes, music, mayhem of the electronic
    sort,
Glimmering from everything arrayed between parenting and religion,
Such martial visions of discrete goals.

Parts of service chanted from ambos, could blur
Because of life's demarcations, spreading chestnut arbors, constituent
    atoms,
Spinning due to computer simulations meant to determine rainfall,
Cups of letters exploded off of pages.

Projects essential to maintaining systematic interaction fail
Despite bright floral carpets studded with burnet, smallage, skirrets,
Generating structural modifications, redefinition, other incalculable help,
Uncommon folk's workaday tapestries.

Chainmail-decked lords, thus get stymied, can't exercise
Although print editors, peer reviews, SEO gurus, all text families,
Array desired properties, create enough expose' for multiple audiences,
Magnetic exchanges juxtaposed with pocket money.

Hand-Powered Ventilators

Hand-powered ventilators, like so many geese chased from corporate
    lawns, or
Comparable to planograms' incipient arguments for placing housewares
    near hosiery,
Seem to exist for purposes suiting the parvenu best.

City parks, chess sets, sandboxes, feral dogs, share contentions, plus lice.
    Otherwise
They occupy crossing guards, eyes fixed on whirling lights, least lucidity
    interrupt clerks'
Orders of eschbeche alongside "Freedom Fries."

Sibilant law makers frequent bondage appointments, act insane when
    named, whine
For hot spots' provision of antimony runcibles, horns borrowed from
    goats, also tails
Used to dress down rascals intent on taking money from the critically ill.

Fire and Rain Running: Saying "No" to an Intimate's Manipulations

Bespeak softly, Dear; see fire and rain running
Jointly insane. Not even your quick cunning
Could have dulled this pain. It's better I explain
Why, when blended, flame plus hail stuns.

Eye Light, Northern Blaze, Sweet Hazy Glow,
Flashing Sentiment, Bane of Darkness, My Heart's Show,
Your bright, coal orbs heat so-so, meet
My needs in part, but beyond your rage, you know

Combined with raindrops, those tears that glisten,
That rioting of viscera makes me listen,
Search, seek, implore for more and better
Means to push away your clouds plus prevent your misting.

Fire plus rain, Darling, dizzies, corrupts, stains,
Water-fed conflagrations, confused parts, remain
Difficult, like acid, send me raving, turn me mad
Heat, water, jiggered together, tend to strain.

Organics' Revelations

Organics reveal too much, expose poor managers, uncover bare claims,
Reveal more than hint about fortunes embedded in mimetic happenstance.

Such rascals harbor, as well, corporate mentations, shelter quixotic notions,
Regard, fondly, fish, fowl, farm-raised flora, espouse sibyl diatribes
     concerning lettuce.

Puerile to a fault, those sops, most visions clotted by government rubrics,
     can't
Help but evolve into altrical administrators, inept clerks, kept mistresses of
     oil barons.

In contrast, children's lunchboxes remain a special sort of juvenile
     hedonism,
Also reason to campaign for increased wages, shiny cars, puppies, plus new
     computers.

No one's wiser from plastic ware when finite nutrition meets federal
     standards,
Processed foodstuffs seem good enough for all sorts of mammon save wild
     politicians.

Labile Lady

The sky, star-paved, watches me.
That vast, avuncular counselor sees
My saturnine coloring, my woad-colored countenance,
Surmises a quaalude commercial on two legs.

Even as I stumble to bruise, she snickers.
Along with her gastropub whores, laughing
Through barking vocals, those counter-melody mavens
Pierce my salacious "sophistication."

Accordingly, heaven spins, spits.
Celestial clarity, starlit understanding fogs
No piker ill with misery, no stingy wage maker
Dares moot rhetoric forward.

Hence, my most ineffable words produce.
Little such spangled magic or tinseled charm brings
Exogenous behaviors, externalized acts
The cosmos quells approbation openly.

Mosquito Bitten

On this thumb, with which I've written,
Many sweet, yet humble rhymes,
I've been wrought and I've been smitten,
There and thus and then each time.

Those wee bits of red on fingers,
Those wee swells of germs on flesh,
Those small mounds of pus that linger,
With each mandible's caress.

I stare. I start. I startle darkly,
Where I bunch with nerves and cry.
I muss. I fuss. I ache yet smartly,
'cause of that uncommon fly.

One bite's the size of Alps in France,
Another raises torturous heat,
I wish a salve, I wish a lance,
Perhaps a cure, or rest replete.

Collect some sedges, lop forb tops,
Just heal my ache; 'twould be fitting,
I'd rejoice when itching stops,
Since I've become mosquito bitten.

Blue

Blue's
Maritime stars,
Maybe, sand dollars,
In concert, spin quickly,
Dance oceanic stirrings, swirl, whisk,
Churn waves, undulate 'til calmer waters
Lull, successfully, such diverse pulses.
Those sines, cosines vie inside
Fields of tangents,
Diagram aqua's
Convolution.

Cycles'
Liquid bubbles,
Globules, almost substance,
Corroborate fishy locals, amid
Turtles, squids, also cetaceans' breathing,
Chasing deep neighborhoods' gill-bearing fiends around.
Meanwhile, short-snouted swimmers snipe, engulf,
Swallow up their friends.
Seas lack heroes;
Food chains
Govern.

Love's
Passing similarity,
Suggests certain complications,
Carries dreadful sacrificing, defeat,
Washes out self-confidence, dims fidelity,
Negates facts even as wet surfaces renew.
Diverse species breed from troubles,
Ooze sludgy, obscure potentials,
Emerge considered optimisms,
Feed, multiply,
Mend.

Triple River City's Cultural Editing

Quintessential blue-collar, triple river cities, like Pittsburgh,
All dragon sight, sound, smell, for the period of high steel production,
Could recite, probably even backwards, data about imports, economies,
The auto industry, war, foreign trade, ethnic neighborhoods,
    simultaneously.

"Speculative fiction" was not so hot as was hard science in the Sputnik/
    Dot.com Era,
During which "slipstream," "steam punk," as well as "urban fantasy," ruled
Private fairytales of six digit-earning dreamers who scratched zits
Despite their pert secretaries, corner offices and access to racquetball
    spas.

Few geeks aligned themselves in ways which opposed nominal
    participation;
Country clubs called more softly than did free lunches, babysitting
    services,
In-house doctors, dry cleaning pickup, also laudatory assemblies
Featuring employs able to improve wireless or other convergent
    conveyances.

Accordingly, social playthings complimented each other, bringing about
Proscribed symmetry, spin, respect for thick glasses, entire complexes
Built of McMansions, a newfound respect for algebra, Latin, sushi,
AP Chemistry, buggy design, salty pretzels, texts sly with algorithms.

Under those conditions, briefly snagging readers' attention meant
Fleshy offerings served up under the guise of: underdog heroes, the fabric
Of animal controllers vanquishing bobcats from northern California
    homes,
Maybe, the esteem captured from graduates from MIT, CMU,
    Northwestern.

These days, authors remain well advised to consider both their immediate
    consumers,
Plus the library patrons who palm phone booth change or pick pockets,
Seeking cell communicators, Star Trek memorabilia, LinkedIn passwords,
Lucky horseshoes, faked bar IDs, stick gum, unused prophylactics.

The transformation of breadwinners from sweats to suits,
Made clear, suddenly, universally, indisputably,
The problem with hybrids, half-baked notions, other mixed bloods.
In industry, like on the farm, mules get trumped by horses.

Spring's Pink and Golden Sunsets

Spring's pink and golden sunsets, her
Ethereal flower bouquets, aerial cotton puffs,
Wadded up cerulean skies, wafting
Perfumed rainbows, low temperatures,
Birds, baby critters, dew-kissed forbs,
Sunset streaks of social networking, elevate.

Until the underbelly of such,
The downside of which, to any monogamous king,
Remains the hard sell of joy, merriment, and splendor,
Among pseudonyms for field behavior, reverted courts,
Hostage taking, opining news sites, switched up guards,
The regular headache of maintaining a treasury, strides forward.

Unfortunately, the need for repudiating nobility has never been remedied.
Chivalrous techniques fail human communication ethics mightily.
Consider that snowy daises, gilded lions, golden loins, peacock jewels,
Sumptuous banquets, bank accounts, banked up follies, parry poorly
Against sunlit histories. Accordingly, many a monarch serves
Beneath azure tapestries, gets fat, cashes in, then dies.

Bodies Roll

Bodies roll, their penurious features compelling more than economic
Platforms. Rather, cultural plateaus get blanketed together by oblates,
    clerks,
Dollar store managers, also anodynes manufactured in garages or in large
    lofts.
They roil for purposes of staying bilious conditions, fallen limbs, and
    rotten teeth.

Putative rabbits breed like nobody's business, their obeisance pain
Expressed in tufts of hair, large litters, maybe also torpid guard dogs.
Consider that when tyros mind the store, beggars' alacrity, pimples, sores,
Like new-fangled protests, make short work of all available social workers.

Those conditions, in turn, encourage the nesting of perspacious eels.
Slithery sorts tend to enjoy flitting among other, lesser, unstable stations.
Seemingly, only conterminously, such invite conflict, upturn civilizations,
Make hazards from twee, worn string, sometimes soggy newspaper logs.

If I were to proposition old goats, seek refuge among picayune heroes, cry
    a bit,
The resulting manners of dance, fireworks, lubricants, would undue me.
(Praetorianism remains underrated except in the lairs of Komodo dragons,
Gray wolves, culpeo foxes, ospreys, goonches, and used car salesmen.)

Morning Song

Good morning blooms, wear your crowns high.
Cup your bright skirts, catch love from the sky.

Good morning trees, stretch for the sun.
Flex each great bough, reach each strong one.

Good morning grass, sway with the wind,
Blades in fast dance, seed heads' swift spin.

Good morning birds, sing from the heart,
Unfurl your wings, expect dumpster cats to eat you.

Susurration

The indistinct sound of people whispering, kneading
"Proper" roles for government, media, public,
Without benefit of actual cartography, even
Eye black, bees wax, paraffin, or carbon.

Once and again words fuel inflammatory powers,
Assuage social prescriptions, descriptions, theories of "the obligatory."
Rather than allow bourgeois meanings to trickle down,
To assign or select, maybe censor, mental sheaves.

Slaves to gist, we shovel our population's fancies,
Cultural traducements, malicious stratifications,
Savoring such chalaques as negates, malevolently,
Any inducements to better wisdoms.

Thereafter, we balk at limits never approached, accepted, acknowledged,
Right ourselves for imaginary moral battles, trump pretend foes,
Cease to be human, desiring, instead, that imperfection directs
Votes, bequeaths leadership, broadcasts saccharine dispersions.

Regimes

A Glossy Coat of Guarantees

A glossy coat of guarantees
Provides no permanent home
For perky political causality.
Affairs of state could improve situations,
Would natural silliness cease, perhaps,
To elate hurt like shepherds castrating sheep.
There's enough gold in these hills for all such fools,
Without their resorting to caustic rhetoric.

Eating broken glass, from time to time,
Sprouts troubles reserved for the likes of axolotls,
Tuataras, and giant salamanders, which, when
Imprisoned in zoological gardens, look
Longingly toward the tree tops, where
Their reptilian eyes alight on habitats occupied
By guans, hammerkops, and whale-headed storks,
Prevented from trafficking with sun or clouds.

Communal affairs would need no handling.
If congregants took care of "the wet stuff;"
Our imagined mansions, jobs, and food bills
Could shrink toward the horizon line,
Restricted, for satisfying durations,
Like so many artists' wares piled up at the souk.
Yet, our public managers elect to transverse clear lines.
We remain governed by alien intentions.

Embrocating Beams

Another new, liberal widow took her former husband's rank in Congress.
There, her pristine disbelief in truck stop values merged with her need for
    votes. Few
Gray-pullers would cede an election to recycling facilities, so she celebrated
    offgrid living.

It seems, often, clout motivates goodwives, moves sibilant objection to the
    aft of ships,
Pushes past resilient regrets, makes headway among tweeting youngsters,
    well-muscled lobbyists.
Thereafter, mercantile dreams beckon with remote possibilities of fame,
    fortune, good hair.

Accordingly, such women never reconstitute their partners' records,
    preferring, instead,
All manner of handmade decorations, stacked planks, carted garbage, new
    monstrances;
Political success remains the province of relatively rigid, parochial
    confederates.

High Floaters' Hardship

Eyrie height, cliffs, trees
Satisfied hunters, except
Those twins sibling-snuffed.

A Skyjacker's Discovery of a Mad Man's Quem

Primitive stone mill prove helpful for grinding thaums by hand.
Verdigris, similarly, is useful when painting gargoyles or coloring in
    henchmen.
Astrolabes, it seems, however, ought to be reserved for other systems'
    denizens.

Short centuries after consulting his clepsydra, he harnessed sufficient
    mental mammals
To demand his neighbor's ancillary chimeras litter elsewhere or yield their
    place in line.
Hungry domestics deserve no leeway least they be spoiled by deprecation.

Contempt's all a mage ought to have needed to dyke up energy particles.
    Except, they're
Times when mad men run their quems into the night. Such operations
    remain dangerous.
Small units, likewise older sorts, run at the first sound of pulverizing. It's
    necessary.

Only goldfish chilled in Champaign bottle, spotted kangaroos, wombats,
    too, survive
Machinations whose unfathomable proportions invite cosmic shuffling.
    Silly beasts.
More common critters, alternatively, remain destined, despite fair kismet,
    to be lunch.

Efforts Otherwise Understood

Ever exasperated with efforts otherwise understood, the tom licked one
  paw.
No single critter, in The True North, or abroad, appreciated his putative
  rationale,
Despite evidence that swallowing field mice headfirst was traditional
  among kin.

As suited select champions, techies, plus additional support staff, all who
  failed mightily,
Getting busted alongside addicts, petty thieves, homicidal wack jobs,
  whores, made news.
Immolation was not usually needed to make weak sorts confess enough to
  build alibis.

Instead, reason jumped past transoms when televised voices repeatedly
  "discovered"
New or large populations worthy of being submitting to second level
  trampling. In realms
Beyond the Arctic, only elves, their fraternal pals, some friends, benefit
  from statutory justice.

Society's Dirty Work

Maintaining a group,
Running stock,
Among daytime's hills and dales,
Interpreting social rules,
As passing fancies compete
Requires deviance.

Goats, unlike lambs,
Would rather wrongly amble,
Than be herded,
For shearing,
Milking,
Or toward the butcher.

Society's dirty jobs,
Get actualized,
One large flock,
After another,
In the quietude,
Of migration's end.

Even so, we work together,
Over great distances,
Supported by wagons,
Self-constructed,
During health checks;
Our hearts were marked.

Death of a Young Boy from the 'Hood: Stratified Healthcare's Disgrace in Serving the General Public

Young farmer boy, fair upon fair,
Young gold on gilded hill,
Counting chaff left from field mining,
Your pale-colored piles tallied,
Wealth-bonded bracts bound homeward.

Bullion plus poor bits, together
At sunset prove nightfall's imminent.
An austere sky's imperfect color
Reveals husks' deficient coinage.
Dusk's loneliness sifts such alchemy money,

Reclaiming all but silver,
When the warehouse journey begins, even ambulance cavalry's
Troubadours, jugglers all red-blue ribboned,
And behemoths decked in bells,
Prove impotent; bankers' hours have finished.

In a day's traffic, few care.
Alabaster carriages come and go, pulling destiny,
Riding provincial chariots
Whose groomsmen carelessly load
Other peoples' riches.

Prosperity makes medical merchants sloppy.
Circumstances, heedless of tomorrows, conspire
Until just one unbolted door
Suffices for gold to slip away, en route,
Entirely wasted.

Elsewhere, common greetings
Plus boxed houses stand,
In reflected glory,
Continuing to ripple
Without their mighty, future glumes.

Delusions of a Hill Shepherd

While memories, of hearth fires or dreams,
Bring simple grass eaters'
Bellyaching songs,
Heather mires those little ground grazers.

Fabricated by deep-eyed knowledge,
Of the universes; perspective on four feet.
Such wee celestial illustrators,
Blanketed solar storms in wild constellations.

Verdant northern pastures'
Sweet bleating looked loving
Toward lowlands where local grasses
Again grazed my ankles to dust.

Nothing spanned their sunshine.
My sheep's action attracted
Just mundane company
Accustomed to windy births.

Matters of cement and asphalt,
Of colorful spaces, whose ill-lit windows
Sifted power from might,
Remained foreign.

When transformed, tainted abalone
Sea shells surround dolphins, sounding
Off on molten morphing unsheathed.
Raw notes blow seaward.

For now, my refugee tent's cups
Lack rice,
In darkness,
I wake wondering.

Wailing Entropy

Flame-shooting dancers'
Most excellent stormed feelings,
Journey 'cross oceans plus
Sands, while reeling with color
Melted from glory songs.

Two simple feathers,
Result in pleasures entranced
By ethereal paths, sometimes
Replete with eternal snow;
No fragmented evidence speaks there.

Humility trembles deviance's demands.
Knowledge's seedlings fail to stand if
Chaos' acumen reigns.
Only blessed herbs wrought and then fraught
With sagacious knowing survive.

At white wisps of whispers,
Chanters dispel troubadours' warnings.
Telling us well where castlers
Can't help civilians any time, any more.
Woe to the wilds!

Pluck reserves for the children,
Denude woodlands for others,
Mothers, fathers, won't/can't stop beasts,
From East of Eden, who meander
Past words yet unspoken, only implored.

Red draws such evening,
Pink cleans those skies,
Mauve tints those shadows,
When rose's whispered nigh.

Green upon laurel,
Olive 'til dim,
Grey upon dusk,
Sunset at a whim,

Myriad light fancies,
Circles of stars,
Thyme, sage, rosemary,
All enthralled from afar.
Warriors' remnants scatter in many lands.

Whose Brutality

On the mountainside,
Where morals slide
Past snowy sheep tethered
To numbered customary behaviors,
Unscrupulous men win.

Their often hidden places,
Locations, where duplicitous faces
Seize citizens marching,
Wobbling past
Yesterday's righteous.

Within familiar mysteries'
Staggering, jagged histories
Form from broken terracotta.
Few remain alive;
Kindnesses get forced.

The hospitality of water snakes,
Stoppages and famine makes
Believers from discontents.
Otherwise, troubled power shifts
To entertain effacing rebels.

Joint Beds

A measure of fame propitiated your favor, perhaps,
Before my placement in depths beneath the tower,
Far from easier routes like couloirs, ice sheets, gorges.

It seems, labdanum, other bewitched perfumes, post pneumonia,
Post coitus, postnominal KC, count nothing against guards,
Serves as meaningless for careful politics, plans, court plots.

We could have joined more than high beds; united entire kingdoms,
Victoriously celebrated, together, our elders' agendas, their land lust,
Reserving coupling as an amusement akin to honeyed snow, opium.

Instead, our coin of minutes, stamped among preterition,
Lost worth as select musicians discretely rewrote scores,
Silked experts, those others preferred the oubliette to passion.

When, finally, the family flautist sneered, proffering execution,
You looked elsewhere, failed to notice my unfurled sleeve, my velvet
Sewn with healing properties like poisoning, impalement, random death.

Women, both princesses and alewives, remain something more than
    chattel.
Narcissistics know nothing of chess, herbal lore, math learned by kings'
    daughters.
So, in the eternities between personal and professional, certain
    boundaries shatter.

A previous span had my nurse reciting ballads, in which prisoners,
Stripped of sovereignty, underfed, maybe raped, spit sibilant notes
Until crystal chanticleers, frenzied clerics, also cavalry, restored order.

Montgolfier Balloons

Hot air vessels, in different circumstances, aeronautics' drays,
Wrap for years in fables, their short sheets draping sofas.
Balloons often get structured from gilded, mud-covered plinths.

All but enlightened enthusiasts are wont to stuff dreams, trash bags,
Rags into their orifices, rant political nonsense, make privileged
Foreclosures, deny that nonpareilles and surfines remain valuable.

Other folk spliflicate; dumbfoundedly, even violently,
Acquire a taste for described suffering, water-absorbent gels,
Handmade refrigerator pictures, the sap of several species.

Perhaps, some would-be partners for urbane entrepreneurs,
Convergent media's corporate potentates, especially in Gotham,
Purport to fill all available nasolabial folds with superglue.

Given their serious fiduciary problems, though, integrated with larger
     foibles,
Those brutes rough out petulant, peevish, sadly fretful texts, get drunk,
Repeatedly "misunderstand" how to cope, culturally, at festivals.

Decadent individuals continue on loath to fly thermal airships.
They reject Kongming lanterns in favor of audio-visual stimulation,
Prefer heavy petitioning to loosening polyurethane sealers.

Whether wrong, immoral, or illegal, comparable starbursts of protective
     coatings,
Boosters' magneto-optic properties aside, provide for parachute vents,
     woven
Rattan, liquid propane, basket lunches, and altimeters formed by
     machine-driven crafting.

Like small children singing prayers for friends before insisting that
    parents allow
Long distance phone calls to camp buddies, overnight marshmallow
    feasts, hedgehog
Pets, pilots, FAA or not, they experience not-so-minute amounts of
    corporeal dissonance.

Areal errors, like stray cats, termites, problematic carpenters,
    telemarketers,
Permeate envelopes, bring greatness begging Wall Street, technique,
    thread, stitch,
Cost maintenance crews long minutes arguing sponsors ignorant of
    paste.

When dilemmas, otherwise, occur postpradinally, yearnings for pelage
    satiations,
No matter how tetchy their instigators, once more becomes the
    collective's norm.
After all, social chitter-chatter can't deter birds, nonstop trips, liftoff,
    ethereal flight.

Privileged Fear

Distinct almost entirely, extinct
Excepting uncharted members,
Save their healthy dread; the hunt.

"Unpreventable" incidents
Regularly precede capture,
Whether mice or men.

Another Win: Political Bedfellows

Tenafly, New Jersey's airport
Pings with presidential hopefuls'
Security detail. Those buzz-cut
Men never suspected that
A fat matron might aim
And fire . . .
At the next president.

Rather than showcase
Ambulance footage, the woman
Locked, currently, on the box
Controlling atom smashers,
Laughed like a criminal.
Cleaning up the party
Proved easier than neutering rabbits.

Only the drug conglomerates sighed
Over loosing their walking billboard
For Viagra. At least the rosy-faced
Opposition remained
Addicted to pain narcotics.
Good 'ol days' elections denied
Chemical barons of vetting opportunities.

Former stump and whistle wars
Brought Lincoln, emancipation, carpet bagging.
Whereas Internet, plus instant messaging, yielded
Contrary perceptions.
America's perceived need for pops and pills
Could still be fanned forever.
Murder makes the vote another win.

I'm So Glad We Took Over: Elitist Politics

It used to be that
The breath and intelligence of life
Explored only rhetorical commands
To answer ingrates.
Nowadays, though,
Learning arrived at "too soon,"
Conflagrates
International incommensurabilities.

Words have begun to swarm
Effects beyond local dominance.
Unimaginable retorts become
Not fictions, but
"Facts on the ground."
Beasts of size no longer seem
Wont to sputter,
Preferring to espouse, instead,

Answers spun past
Political apparati.
Commonplace casualties
Yelp toward our media's
Voyeuristic lens, mirroring,
"Idealism," while not surely building
Truths understood
By society's top or bottom.

Such enviable texts embrace,
Like rows of tangled eyelashes;
They vibrate vacantly as their
Sound bites substitute
Authentic conceits, where convenient,
For compounded, nasty
Tendencies in governance.
I'm so glad we took over.

Conduits

Intergalactic Balladeer

I'm an intergalactic balladeer.
Singing shanties for gelatinous monsters, crying
Over the bowdlerization of abandoned space shuttles.

So many preceptors, their arachnoids hanging out like ripe fruit,
Whose delicate membranes once enclosed spinal cords, brains,
    undeveloped
Viscera awash in stargazing captains' pipe dottle, routed from conflict.

Retreat's become sexier than Fibonacci series poetry, truncated finals or
    encroaching
Territories where, even unwittingly, social alluvium's allowed;
Seeding one's self in such systems makes orators' agitprop famous.

Where we see blood, audiences merely evidence aggravated cases of
    tonsillitis.
That's okay; runty aliens, possessed of menial market mendacities, gills,
    fins,
Plus other useful parts shrive their respiration fatigue upon us bipeds.

In balance, our quisling experiences yield famous moral skirmishes.
Low content, high drama's what brings sell outs. Slavery, worse tortures
    constitute
Fun and games for payday squads of andouille-hankering reptiles.

Their future's a precious caper-type berry of sun-starved gorse.
Some species can't know the ennui of kind deeds, reliable agreements or
    permanent
Mates. They remain on empty vestas, those protoplanet denizens devoid
    of pleasure.

Such masses, however, are more gratifying than cosmos construed of
    bulbs,
Flashes, solar capucines, deep rubies, bright feathers.
Accordingly, I snooze in my cockpit, electronic pen ready.

Spring

Meadow flowers reach.
Raptors sing robins' music.
Tree blossoms witness.

That Hard or Fibrous Center

That hard or fibrous center, where tomorrow's promises rest protected
From infantile attempts to control the contours of life,
Relies on words, tears, even borrowed truths to liberate
Ventricles from blockage, brains from malfunction.

Sure, the shin bone's connected to the ankle while
Backaches blossom from muscular ailments, leaving stressors innocent.
It might also be the case that it's wise to keep hedgehogs as pets,
At least until morning or until all cockroaches and silver fish are eaten.

Extended family's travesties remain reachable through local libraries,
Plus, more recently, via Internet PDF files as well as by LinkedIn and
    Facebook.
Recall, suaedas and cacti, alike, can perish in sustained drought, worms,
    sometimes,
Are bait, not compost machines. There are mornings not worth greeting,

In systems seemingly free of green toilets, it's still possible to link liberal
Views on fur usage to current, proper mechanics for simple sentences.
Anarchy's fingertips might touch, freedom, health, tolerance,
But bedbugs needn't upset apple carts enough to actualize change.

Pit Bulls plus Pigeons

Pit bulls plus pigeons, not in civil units, alone, used terms so provocative
As to be considered squicky among species. They released personal truths which
Favored homebody leftovers, baize better spread beneath billiards, and personal glory.

The range of ways in which persons justified cross-phyletic information,
Brought explicit causuistric data sufficiently disturbing as to thwart lovers' calumnies,
To screwpull corks, to mess with echolalic, well-aimed jests, and to confuse adolescents.

Once our convergent media found its perigee, uncanny prurience filled bandwidths.
While cycloptic sources conveyed species' guttering, Pay Pal accounts bled dry.
Juke along little doogie or you'll die.

Penguins in Periwigs

Penguins in Periwigs, tumbling dominos on Planet Izakaya,
Let loose screed so cacophonous that gelatinous beasts cry.
Those viscous critters, in turn, overmix some boiling sludge;
They douse their transparent dormice.

Achievements' relative merit rests on perception
Plus on radar-registered printouts of inaccessible galaxies.
Everyone sings at captains' tables; truth being
No one wants termite salad or sapote tea on the long haul.

Besides, most brutes recite poems in which *anthriscus* is more than a
    solvent;
They recall commercial blood cleansing booths featuring chervil twice daily.
Sometimes debris-ridden organisms feel refreshed thereafter.
Otherwise, they party on, singing karaoke with wigged, but svelte, water
    fowl.

Encomia

Errant encomia;
Eminent elocutions
Encircle unduly.

Between Tradition and Deviance on a
New Jersey Highway

Between Routes 609 and 43,
My car stalled more than motion.
Trapped between pinafores and "yes sirs,"
Yet, wanting no part of briefcases,
Jogging shoe outlets, or soccer fields,
I slowed to park.

Glossies with bouffant hairdos,
Lesbian books of letters, plus
Soiled diapers guarded our chassis,
While we ambulated across colored daisies.
The baby's Snuggie swung
Amid tack country and city life.

Retired RVers waved down
Our caravan, every one
Military husbands,
White shoes, straw hats.
Then looked away, regarded
Lawns, fat dogs, cement storefronts.

My toddler's tears returned me
To gas station needs,
Convenience stores, payphones.
The baby's howl, too,
Reminded, with prescience,
About highway nights.

A tow truck later,
Some chewing gum,
A guilty chocolate,
Home hung the horizon.
Alley cat ideas, all *a cappella*,
Remained at the meridian.

Moving a Divorcee and Her Kids across State Lines

The time was five-thirty,
I woke with a start;
Something was following
My mama's sure cart.
Shifting from "park" to "drive,"
She toggled to speed,
Pumped hard on the gas,
Mom gave little heed.

Behind us a mammoth,
A terror in measure,
With hinged, metal wings,
Which held fast to our treasure
The bulk of that weirdness,
Its preponderance,
Approached our back bumper,
Threatened to compress.

Mom dove and she darted,
She jumped lanes at great pace,
Yet that overgrown beasty
Well matched our pure haste.
With lights like grand eyeballs,
A windshield as mouth,
It adamantly tailgated
Three states to the south.

Then, deep into the night
In a neighborhood new
With that monster behind us,
We kids did construe
A federal license
A driver or more,
Our cash, our possessions,
The complete "country store."

They'd been able to link
Our past life to the present,
Had managed to help
Make our changeover pleasant.
With wide eyes we watched
The wine being poured
As cartons and boxes
Transversed our front porch.

Erudition

Erudition costs big figs,
Sometimes takes funding, otherwise earmarked
For affection and romantic love.

At farmers' markets, counterculture wisdom sells
Like blueberry muffins or gladiolas.
Hillsmen set great store by second-hand furnishings.

Bleak Ranger

Dream of crystal castles, think on clouds in cold, crisp air.
Be mesmerized by ice flakes; when they're falling, I'll appear.
Hold fast to ivory towers, imagine rapture, shade-pierced skies,
Believe in magic stories, whose small words threshold you and I.
Latch tight to wild zephyrs, summon them around your face,
Gather quickly all stray sun beams, nobly rid them from your space.
Our love can't bloom like flowers; there's no good sentiment in mirth,
My heart yields no fiery bower, never claimed a heated hearth. Not possible.

But for your troth, I'll risk nights past the snow;
Chance your fair bed while the fronds start to grow.
Such paradise's odd among old, hoarfrosted things,
There's rarely witnessed such worship in shadowy flings.
Day star, sweet light, creature born to the sun,
Even so, with time, your cost, more than elsewise will run
Me away from your nidus, your jacaranda tree,
The seasons of flame remain fatal to me.

After Centuries, the Air Still Felt of Death

Dark air, cold mist, raw meat, stench, boldness ribboning truculent blades.
Scurrilous women bark, make foggy breath, strip corpses of linen, gold, wine.

Elsewhere, cars chase similar scenes, knock innocents over, morph lives, splay
Copses of trees to firewood, celebrate the advent of mechanical over human.

Another Wave-Washed Fire Opal in Hollywood

Two beach glass pebbles with shared chromosomes,
Watched high tides scoring our childhood home,
Yet Malibu lightning leaves you suffering alone;
We're segmented by the salt and the sea.

Gilded gift wrappings suppress actual needs,
Tiffany fixtures, gin, fog memories,
Unlisted numbers quell quieted deeds;
I'm mere words on an answering machine.

Lush wardrobes bait ineffectual dreams,
Parents' view becomes graft of esteem,
Plus purchased embrasures make integrity lean;
You shore up our compromised family tree.

Kissy-faced strangers pander you utterly,
Mirrored distortions, their discourse is southerly,
They hunt your fine treasures, want your money's certainty;
They're happy to hide truth below shorelines dutifully.

When happens that funeral, to unanswered love,
Measured enlightenment cancels wisdoms above,
Ethos' revival looses when purchased friends' provide song;
Just my eye water's left to cover your stone.

Abseiling from Dreams in TV Land

Theodore thought carefully before
Abseiling from dreams.
It remained insufficient to repel
Down beyond nightmares;

He meant to descend, instead,
Leaving a fantasy, in which no less than sixty
Million women wanted him,
Sitting quietly in their prairie houses.

A steep drop,
Versus his daytime popularity,
Would have troubled the troubadour
Enough to break somnolence.

He'd have awakened sobbing,
A breathless balladeer at rope's end,
Minus a knot or other constructive device
By which to climb back.

To wit, he flattening against
Fandom's vertical cliff. The man
Sucked in gut and hope,
Exerted himself

Forward until plummeting
Toward an improved, spectacular ending.
After all, such diva curtain calls mean
Certain posthumous success.

Except for Guests, Who Fill up Seats: Media Watch

Except for guests, who fill up seats,
We record every rich or savory face.
Our station makes reservations with social nuance.

Here, flavorful electronic bits stuff, delight us while false accusations
Feed opulent persons (through flashy news services) and
Buffet our skunky attitudes higher.

Beyond such choice tables, folks fork fame for small fortunes.
Alternatively, pay verdant fees for raw publicity spiced with fire.
Worldwide aromatic events are known to kill select couplings.

Consider, wrongness, her sisters, her auntie, also her dad,
Seeped hotly inside Bollywood, that's Mumbai's, cauldrons until
Various likenesses plated up bitterness.

Sometimes, their promised, florescent ramifications, settled generations
Without causing indigestion or categorical annoyances.
Other times, related mouthfeel accentuated scandal, horror and loss.

Biblical mores evoke stares, cause burps, and dirty polite serviettes,
But sagacious paths, unlike mediated charm, lead to good decisions.
It's useful to reevaluate convergent image streams and to salt our words.

Nibbled to Death by Ducks and Other
Useless Pithy Sayings

The problem with hybrids is horses trump mules,
Intergalactic life's not merely fiction, also, hedgehogs bite.
Coaxing a vegetable patch into productivity
Means, most often, foregoing rewriting habits.
Plus, it's long been vain and entirely foolish
To somaticize misogyny among members of the track and field team.

The need to challenge social supremacy evolved because
Butterfly gardens, even when surrounded by large sunbeams,
Couldn't transform worms into compost factories or switch up
Manure's value. Simply, throwing breakfast cereal around, in Ivy League
    halls,
Remained underrated, causing too many thinkers' to get packed
    permanently.
Hegemonic justice still reinstates overseers long before hazy morals clear.

Alternatively, owning a new car beats getting by with bus passes.
Such transportation invalidates contentions that my husband's tribe raids
    boarders;
New schedules, not to mention transfers and correct change flummox
    them.
There are no fiduciary incentive known to man, which manage to reassure
Young ark raider that theropods, as shown in museums, movies, YouTube,
Are other than images conjured by Nineteenth Century amateurs.

Sadly, more vapid than flying squirrels, some parents yet foam over
    acceptance letters
From name brand schools, employers fixated on future means, marriage
    partners.
Sending junior off to venues where the quiddity of social climbing is learnt
Where smart moles understand that it's briskly refreshing to offer
    contritions
Provides enough tripe, blather, other assorted nonsense to bring
Dialectic so insufferable as to call up all manner of *anatidae*.

Those feathery fellows, in turn, happily make frotteunstic victims out of
    youths
Or consort with unsuspecting humans bedecked, in jewels' flavorful
    fashions.
Finding it insufficient purely to abide the forensics of boarding schools,
Certain aquatic birds struggle free from words' imperfections,
Sway, then heave green-backed remedies for addiction, depression,
    inheritance.
Select loons, grebes, coots, known for adolescents' erudition, peck.

Dabbling ducks, it seems, feed mainly by upending. They've no remorse
    over
Deconstructing familial expectations. In spite of everything, small town
    registers
Know nothing of critical thinking, of creative approaches, of using
    intellect rather
Than slouching through with social clout. Personal needs, in light of
    intergenerational
Strictures, revert folly, push human habituation toward boorish fratire,
Save for when ducklings refuse stony asteroids and domestication.

Conclusion: Bucking at Social Mores

Institutions change but slowly;
Anomie's not grown
From jailhouse youth,
Or propagated by rural attics.
Insolently, most social weaknesses arrive
Within folks which conformity's failed to figure.

Such emotionally estranged, maybe even closeted
Persons, ignorant of collective "advancements,"
Mistakenly beholden themselves to custom
Until they're incarcerated.
Their obliviousness is our fault;
We, the citizens, raised the limbo pole.

Communal behavior, upheld by most minions,
In times of war, famine, (Or, for elite,
During economic uncertainty or further threats to power),
Discredits people missing cooperative camouflage.
Alienation, isolation and loss pervade the underground.
Like fetid perfume, they're reciprocally rancid.

Instinctively, we move such champions
To the "nonstandard" column, where
Comprehensive reform promises enlightenment.
Thereafter, our safety gets reinforced by media campaigns.
It's tough to abide the flagrant disregard of moral
Strictures, to witness freedom from convention.

Cowardliness remains a popular fashion.
Shared vulnerability withstands no
"Passing;" schoolchildren realize heroes' bread
Often tastes salty, given the requisite tears. Such dough
Hurts more than rough-won trophies awarded for turning in
Varmints; long range hunting still best suits us.

Credits

"A Glossy Coat of Guarantees." *Mad Swirl*. Jul. 2011.

"A Grand Sociology Lesson" as "A Quick Sociology Lesson." *Bewildering Stories*. Feb. 2010.

"A Skyjacker's Discovery of a Mad Man's Quem." *BRICKrhetoric*. May. 2011.

"Abseiling from Dreams in Hollywood." *Callused Hands*. Jan. 2010.

"After Centuries, the Air Still Felt of Death." *Danse Macabre*. Aug. 2012.

"All Manner of Rebellion." *Certain Circuits*. Apr. 2012.

"An Adolescent's Didactic Lament: Round Pegs, Square Holes." *Spark!* Sep. 2010.

"Another Wave-Washed Fire Opal in Hollywood." *Winamop*. Dec. 2010.

"Another Win: Political Bedfellows." *Word Salad Online*. Oct. 2012.

"Anteros' Celadon Whirligig: A Lecturer's Antique Lament." *vox poetica*. Nov. 2012.

"Australian Kennels." *The Blue and Yellow Dog*. Spring 2012.

"Autoethnographic Writing Down Under." *Cantaraville*. Oct. 2009. 172-173.

"Because of a Woodland View." *Danse Macabre*. Jul. 2012.

"Bent Reeds." *Danse Macabre*. May 2012.

"Between Tradition and Deviance on a New Jersey Highway." *The Camel Saloon*. Mar. 2012.

"Bleak Ranger." *Danse Macabre*. Nov. 2011.

"Blue." *Spark!* Dec. 2013.

"Bodies Roll." *Winamop*. Mar. 2013.

"Bucking at Social Mores." *Bewildering Stories*. Jan. 2011.

"Certain Parameters." *Mad Swirl*. Dec. 2013.

"Civilization's 'Little Words.'" *The Camel Saloon*. Apr. 2012.

"Current Regard for the Newly Not-so-Rich." *Soft Whispers*. Apr. 2010.

"Death of a Young Boy from the 'Hood: Stratified Healthcare's Disgrace in Serving the General Public." *Spark!* May 2010.

"Delusions of a Hill Shepherd." *Ken*Again*. Dec. 2008.

"Eat Merrily: A Little Girl's Cacophonous Tastes." *vox poetica*. Mar. 2011.

"Efforts Otherwise Understood." *BRICKrhetoric*. May. 2011.

"Embrocating Beams." *BRICKrhetoric*. Aug. 2012.

"Encomia." *Danse Macabre*. Aug. 2011.

"Erudition," *Bewildering Stories*. Jan. 2010.

"Except for Guests Who Fill up Seats: Media Watch." *Stride Magazine*. Nov. 2009.

"Fame." *Ken*Again*. Jun. 2011.

"Fifty Is Years Old Enough." *vox poetica*. Sep. 2012.

"Fire and Rain Running: Saying 'No' to an Intimate's Manipulations." *Mad Swirl*. Aug. 2011.

"Forget Elastic." *The Voices Project*. Sep. 2013.

"Fug Music." *Danse Macabre*. Oct. 2012.

"Given a Chair." *The Camel Saloon*. Sep. 2011.

"Hand-Powered Ventilators." *The Camel Saloon*. Jan. 2012.

"Hardly any Cosmic Answers at the Universe's Hub." *Danse Macabre*. Apr. 2012.

"He Thrives While I'm Exsanguinated." *The Mind[less] Muse*. Dec. 2012.

"High Floaters' Hardship." *The Camel Saloon*. Nov. 2011.

"If Birds were to be Believed." *Mad Swirl*. Feb. 2012.

"Ill-Planned Legacies." *Social-i Magazine*. Dec. 2010. 14.

"I'm So Glad We Took Over." *Bewildering Stories*. Jan. 2010.

"I'm so Hungry I Could Sing About It: Empty of Love and Money." *Bewildering Stories*. Nov. 2013.

"Intergalactic Balladeer." *Bewildering Stories*. Nov. 2012.

"Israeli Jasmine." *The Camel Saloon*. Aug. 2011.

"Joint Beds." *vox poetica*. Nov. 2012.

"Little Mustangs among Older Friends." *Mused-the Bella Online Literary Review*. Dec. 2010.

"Mama's Mundane Witnessing." *Bewildering Stories*. Sep. 2011.

"Morning Song." *Danse Macabre.* Oct. 2012.

"Mosquito Bitten." *The Ranfurly Review*. Jun. 2011.

"Moving a Divorcee and Her Kids across State Lines." *Mad Swirl*. Nov. 2011.

"My Backyard Squirrels." *Sarasvati*. Jan. 2010.

"Neighborhood Nuisances through Cats' Eyes." *Winamop*. May 2012.

"Nibbled to Death by Ducks." *BRICKrhetoric*. Aug. 2011.

"On Her Birthday, That Threshold of First Roses." *vox poetica*. Jul. 2012.

"Pamela's Poem: Cabbage and Milk Thistle." *Riverbabble*. Jan. 2014.

"Past the Halflings' Village." *Bewildering Stories*. May 2010.

"Penguins in Periwigs." *Stride Magazine*. Nov. 2009.

"Piaget's Sagacity" *Etc: A Review of General Semantics*. 2013. 70.1. 72-73.

"Pit Bulls plus Pigeons." *Bewildering Stories*. May 2011.

"Privileged Fear." *vox poetica*. Jan. 2014.

"Regard Carefully." *Winamop*. Sep. 2014.

"'Retarded:' Another Spoil of Child Abuse." *Ygdrasil*. May 2013.

"Rorschach Blot Interpreted by an Automated Man." *Aoife's Kiss*. Dec. 2011. 61.

"Round, Pop, Shout." *Mad Swirl*. Jun. 2014.

"School Norms: Innocents Enough to be Eaten Alive." *Fallopian Falafel*. Jun. 2011. 57.

"Society's Dirty Work." *JMWW*. Jul. 2010.

"Some Cranium Treasures Sit Derelict: Reasons to be Mindful of Children." *vox poetica*. Nov. 2011.

"Spring." *Bewildering Stories*. Mar. 2011.

"Spring's Pink and Gold Sunsets." *Danse Macabre*. Aug. 2011.

"Sticky Feasts ought not to be Second-rate." *Haggard and Halloo*. Aug. 2012.

"Stroppy Urchins." *The Camel Saloon*. Sep. 2011.

"Susurration." *Mad Swirl*. Jul. 2012.

"Telephone Love of Decades Past (A Carol)." *The Camel Saloon*. Oct. 2011.

"Term Choice." *The Strand Book of International Poets*. Eds. Imran Hanif and Jane Lee. Strand Publishing. 2010. 56.

"That Hard or Fibrous Center." *Gypsy Daughter's Brown Bagazine*. Jun. 2011. 16-17.

"The Amusement Park among the Steel Mills: Reminiscing over Pittsburgh." *Danse Macabre*. Sep. 2010.

"The Boondoggles of Debt: A Contemporary Lament." *SPENDonLIFE.com*. Sep. 2009.

"The Empyrean, Principality of Young Ages." *Mad Swirl*. Nov. 2012.

"The Fullness of Aging: Autumn's Showy Bounty." *vox poetica*. Dec. 2011.

"The Pantyhose Horrors of Summer Internships." *The Camel Saloon*. Dec. 2012.

"The Smell of Water." *The Blue and Yellow Dog*. Spring 2012.

"Thelma's Nursing Home." *The New Aesthetic*. Feb. 2011.

"Triple River City's Cultural Editing." *Winamop*. Jan. 2012.

"Tuesday Night at the Student Union." *Sarasvati*. Jan. 2010.

"Unemployment's Huffs and Puffs." *The Camel Saloon*. Oct. 2011.

"Versey: The Wilds of Advertising." *Fowl Feather Review*. Feb. 2015.

"Wailing Entropy." *Halfway Down the Stairs*. Mar. 2010.

"Whose Brutality." *The Camel Saloon*. Jun. 2012.

Acknowledgments

Maybe middle-aged gals ought to utter only niceties, but literature, which reflects veracity, must also contain reprehensible sentiments. Hence, I remain indebted to my family and friends, whom tolerate the nefarious stuff I produce alongside of words fashioned from sweetness and light. Accordingly, I extend warm thanks to my husband, to my children, and to my tenacious prickle of imaginary hedgehogs.

Author Bio

KJ Hannah Greenberg has been too busy parenting her emerging adult sons and daughters to contemplate her navel. Add to the mix two grandbabies, and it seems unlikely she'll ever proceed in a straightforward manner. If she had five extra minutes, she would bake quinoa pie and feed it to her imaginary hedgehogs. Meantime, she steals sleep and laughs. On rare, alternate Tuesdays, Hannah and her furz-pigs fly the galaxy in search of adventures.

Two decades ago, while focused on her children, Hannah eked out: a novel, a ream of poetry, and a couple of cute, creative nonfiction pieces that referenced the "growth opportunities" concomitant to parenting. However, Hannah stored those treasures, rather than offering them up for publication, since she was busy mopping carpets, diapering doll bottoms, and chopping beans. Meanwhile, to distract herself from the less pleasant moments of motherhood, she taught calculus to high school students and conducted university classes in Argumentation and Debate, Interpersonal Communication, and Feminist Sociology. Hannah holds both a B.S. in Technical (Science) Writing and Editing from Carnegie-Mellon University and a PhD in Rhetoric from The University of Massachusetts.

When Hannah and her family relocated to "the other side of the world," her life changed. Specifically, when Hannah was entertaining some female friends with a tall tale about falafel balls, preteen fashion sense, and "special American pricing," she was told: to keep her hot sauce to herself, to realign her skirt, and to return to writing.

A multi-year stint blogging about intercultural communication, for *The Jerusalem Post*, followed as did a few months of teaching chemistry and of discovering that the local, dumpster cats were really "squirrels." Hannah edited a paper, for a Weizmann Institute scientist, on the effects of electrical stimulus on the hippocampus, and diffidently wrote and published a handful of stories in places such as *Mishpacha's Calligraphy* and *MidCentury Modern Moms*. She also bought a pair of very large earrings. Additionally, Hannah judged creative nonfiction for *Notes & Grace Notes*, became a "Poet of the Week" at *Poetry Super Highway* and developed Expressively Yours Writing Workshops of Jerusalem.

During the summer of 2008, at last sufficiently frustrated with her inability to locally lecture on discourse, Hannah rededicated her verbal zest to distant points. Specifically, she dusted off her keyboard and began to churn out more smoothies, vegetable soup, and creative works than might be considered proper for a middle-aged mom.

By 2009, Hannah began blogging for the USA's *Type-A Parent*, wrote a column for the UK's *The Mother Magazine*, and served as an Associate Editor at both *Sotto Voce* and *Bewildering Stories*. She received her first Pushcart Prize nomination that year.

2010 found Hannah writing monthly critiques for *Tangent*, the speculative fiction review, and blogging for Australia's *Kindred*. That year, too, *Oblivious to the Obvious: Wishfully Mindful Parenting*, a collection of her humorous essays, was published by French Creek Press.

In 2011, Hannah became an Associate Editor at *Bound Off*, began writing about Judaism for *The Jerusalem Post*, brought her creative writing workshops to the Association of Americans and Canadians in Israel, and joined the lineup at *Natural Jewish Parenting*. She received her second Pushcart

Prize nomination and celebrated the publication of *A Bank Robber's Bad Luck with His Ex-Girlfriend*, a poetry collection, by Unbound CONTENT.

2012 was the year that four of Hannah's books were published; the first edition of *Don't Pet the Sweaty Things*, a short fiction collection, was offered by Bards & Sages Publishing; *Fluid & Crystallized*, a poetry chapbook, was issued by Fowlpox Press; Supernal Factors, a poetry chapbook, went public thanks to The Camel Saloon Books on Blog; and *Intelligence's Vast Bonfires*, a poetry collection, by Lazarus Media, too, got sold. As well, in 2012, Hannah was nominated for The Best of the Net.

In 2013, Hannah's *Citrus-Inspired Ceramics*, a poetry collection, was published by Aldrich Press. Plus, and the first edition of *The Immediacy of Emotional Kerfuffles*, a short story collection, was released by Bards & Sages Publishing. Hannah was nominated for the Million Writers Award, and was nominated, for a third time, for the Pushcart Prize. Furthermore, Hannah brought her writing workshops to the OU Israel Center in Jerusalem, began to offer annual writing retreats, taught an advanced course in book writing and publishing, and began to teach long distance courses.

In 2014, three of Hannah's books were published; the poetry collection, *The Little Temple of My Sleeping Bag*, by Dancing Girl Press, the poetry chapbook, *Dancing with Hedgehogs*, by Fowlpox Press, and the second edition of the short story collection *Don't Pet the Sweaty Things*, by Bards & Sages Publishing. What's more, Hannah led another writing retreat in Tzfat, and again offered face-to-face writing courses in her home.

2015 found Hannah leaving behind blogging to focus on book writing. Among her publications that year were: *Cryptids*, by Bards & Sages Publishing, the second edition of *The Immediacy of Emotional Kerfuffles*, also by Bards & Sages Publishing, *Jerusalem Sunrise*, an essay collection, by Imago Press, and *Word Citizen: Uncommon Thoughts on Writing, Motherhood & Life in Jerusalem*, an essay collection, by Tailwinds Press. As well, Hannah offered Internet courses on the Elements of Literature, including: Character Development, Plot Development, Dialogue, Descriptive Writing, and Tone. For a fourth time, she was nominated for the Pushcart

Prize. One of Hannah's brief fictions was named Best Story of the Year by *Calliope*, MENSA's literary magazine, too.

In 2016, Bards & Sages Publishing will offer another of Hannah's story collections, *Friends and Rabid Hedgehogs*, Broken Publications will issue a collection of Hannah's nonfiction, *The Nexus of The Sun, The Moon, and Mother*; and UnboundCONTENT will present a poetry collection of Hannah's, *Mothers Ought to Utter Only Niceties*. Meanwhile, Hannah will continue offering Internet writing workshops on topics such as: Rewriting, Style, and Audience.

Also by KJ Hannah Greenberg

Prose

The Nexus of The Sun, The Moon, and Mother (Broken Publications, 2016, Forthcoming)

Friends and Rabid Hedgehogs (Bards and Sages Publishing, 2016, Forthcoming)

Cryptids (Bards and Sages Publishing, 2015)

Jerusalem Sunrise (Imago Press, 2015)

Word Citizen (Tailwinds Press, 2015)

The Immediacy of Emotional Kerfuffles, 2nd ed. (Bards and Sages Publishing, 2015)

Don't Pet the Sweaty Things, 2nd ed. (Bards and Sages Publishing, 2014)

Oblivious to the Obvious: Wishfully Mindful Parenting (French Creek Press, 2010) Conversations on Communication Ethics (Praeger, 1991)

Watercolors (Scotch & Soda Productions, 1979)

Poetics

Mothers Ought to Utter Only Niceties (Unbound CONTENT, 2016, Forthcoming)

Dancing with Hedgehogs (Fowlpox Press, 2014)

The Little Temple of My Sleeping Bag (Dancing Girl Press, 2014)

Citrus-Inspired Ceramics (Aldrich Press, 2013)

Supernal Factors (The Camel Saloon Books on Blog, 2012)

Fluid & Crystallized (Fowlpox Press, 2012)

A Bank Robber's Bad Luck with His Ex-Girlfriend (Unbound CONTENT, 2011)

www.ingramcontent.com/pod-product-compliance
Lightning Source LLC
Chambersburg PA
CBHW071349090426
42738CB00012B/3060